D1608345

**CLASSIC RECIPES, FROM
BAKLAVA TO FIG ICE CREAM**

sweet middle east

Anissa Helou

Photographs by Linda Pugliese

CHRONICLE BOOKS
SAN FRANCISCO

For my friend Ilaria and my brother Joseph, who have been instrumental in my successful transition from the art world to the food world.

Library of Congress Cataloging-in-Publication Data available.

ISBN 978-1-4521-1439-2

Manufactured in China

Designed by Alice Chau
Photographs by Linda Pugliese
Food styling by Chelsea Zimmer
Prop styling by Kira Corbin

The photographer wishes to thank her dedicated team—Chelsea Zimmer, Kira Corbin, Julia Gartland, Leslie Gordon, and Sophie Leng—for all their hard work and support. She would also like to thank Alice Chau for her trust and collaboration.

10 9 8 7 6 5 4 3 2 1

Chronicle Books LLC
680 Second Street
San Francisco, California 94107
www.chroniclebooks.com

contents

introduction

I have a strong sweet tooth and I often say it's because my family name, Helou, means "sweet" in Arabic. In truth, that has nothing to do with it. Most people in the Middle East and North Africa have a serious penchant for all things sugary. Sweets occupy an important place in our lives, and every important occasion, rite of passage, or religious event has a specific sweet associated with its celebration. In fact, any occasion is a good enough reason to visit the sweets maker, whether to enjoy a snack while going about your daily business or to buy a treat to take to friends or family.

It's possible that this love of sweet things is a result of the Muslim prohibition against alcohol, with sugar from sweets replacing the sugar derived from alcohol. Perhaps sugar (from the Arabic word *sukkar*, derived from the Persian *shakar*) was so plentiful in the Middle East that a tradition of candy and pastry making was established. Sugarcane was originally grown in the tropical Far East; from there it was taken to India and China and on to Persia in the fifth century. After the Arabs invaded Persia in the seventh century they carried sugar with them to Egypt, North Africa, Sicily, Spain, and other places they conquered. When the Crusaders left the Middle East, they brought sugar with them back to Europe. Sugar was not the only sweetener available in the Middle East (honey and molasses from grapes, dates, and carob were and still are used as well), though it was plentiful there long before sugar became common in the West.

The sugar industry started in Egypt in the eighth century, and the Egyptians were considered pioneers in refining sugar. They're still major growers and producers of sugar, with more than three hundred million acres given over to growing sugarcane, which does not include the land on which sugar beets are grown. Iran is another country with an important sugarcane growing and refining industry.

Sweets are an essential part of the legendary Middle Eastern and North African hospitality, and they are ever-present in people's homes, stored in beautiful glass or metal boxes and placed on coffee tables in living rooms so hosts can offer them to guests with coffee, tea, or a refreshing drink. *Everyone* brings a gift when invited to someone's home, and sweets are often what visitors bring with them.

Wherever you go in the region, whether in the souks, bazaars, or the modern parts of cities, you find confections of all kinds. Some are piled high on carts by the roadside, others delicately arranged on huge metal trays in the shops of sweets makers. Don't assume that sweets sold on the street aren't as good as those displayed in elegant stores. Some may be of lesser quality, but others will have been lovingly prepared by the vendors in their homes and match those available at the finest shops.

Most people in the Levant still cook elaborate meals at home, though few home cooks prepare their own desserts, even if they know how. In North Africa, home cooks are very proud of their pastry-making skills. Apart from a few sweets such as *ma'mul* (see page 56) and various puddings that are considered the preserve of the home cook, most Levantines buy their desserts and pastries from specialty shops—just as many French and Italians do. In the Middle East and North Africa, however, these delicacies are enjoyed not so much for dessert at the end of the meal, when fruit is usually served, but rather for breakfast or between meals with coffee or tea.

As a child in Beirut, I often went with my mother or sometimes my father to buy sweets, simply as a treat for us to have at home or to take to my grandmother who lived in East Beirut, the Christian part of the city. We lived in West Beirut, the Muslim part, and it was there that all the great confectioners had their stores. They were mainly Muslim, with many having been in the business for generations. In the 1960s when I was growing up there, the most famous were the Samadis and the Bohsalis in Beirut and the Hallabs in Tripoli (the last two are still going strong, though Samadi Sweet Shop may have lost its shine). I speculate that most confectioners are Muslims because Christians had to be austere during the forty days of Lent. Muslims, on the other hand, enjoyed a feast every night during Ramadan (the Muslim month of fasting), with sweets taking center stage throughout that month as well as for the feast celebrating the end of Ramadan, Eid al-Fitr (known as Şeker Bayramı, Sugar Feast, in Turkey), and the even bigger feast a month or so later, Eid al-Adha. Christians celebrate with sweets as well, especially at Easter, but not so extravagantly.

What I never noticed when I lived in Beirut was the lack of access to the confectioners' kitchens. It was never a problem peeking into restaurant kitchens or watching bakers at work, but it wasn't until I started writing about food that I realized I had never been inside any sweets-makers' kitchens. That mysterious world was out-of-bounds to everyone except professionals. The very first time I visited Güllüoğlu's baklava kitchens in Istanbul, it felt like walking into an enchanted world: everything was cloaked in clouds of white dust (created by the cornstarch, which is used to keep the phyllo from sticking as it is rolled out). Men in white moved gracefully and dexterously, rolling out incredibly large, diaphanous sheets of phyllo dough, which they then flapped one by one before laying them on large metal trays, building layers interspersed with chopped nuts to make different types of baklava.

Later, I was fortunate enough to be allowed inside the kitchens of Pistache d'Alep in Aleppo, and there I finally discovered the art of making cotton candy (*ghazl al-banat* in Arabic), an extraordinary confection made by stretching caramel and coating it with toasted flour. As the caramel is stretched again and again, it separates into millions of incredibly fine strands that are then coiled into balls that melt on your tongue as you eat them, as if you were eating sweet air. Later still, I visited the kitchens of İmam Çağdaş in Gaziantep in southeastern Turkey, where the atmosphere was positively medieval. The wood fire in the oven cast a warm orange glow over the men, who made the baklava "dance" by pouring hot syrup over it. The syrup made the top layers of phyllo bob up and down, though never strongly enough to fly off the tray.

The repertoire of sweets is vast, from puddings to syrupy pastries to cookies to ice creams to candied fruit, nuts, and even some vegetables such as eggplant. From these I have chosen an exciting selection of recipes that can be made by amateur home cooks. The satisfaction of making a perfect *m'hanncha*, or almond spiral (or even an imperfect one), is empowering; serving your own homemade ice cream allows you to experiment with unusual flavors and combinations as well as impress whoever is lucky enough to eat it; and the cook will, like the best leavened pastry, puff up with pride.

Some ingredients may not be readily available in supermarkets, but you will have no problem finding them online or at specialty stores (see Sources, page 162). And most of these ingredients have a long shelf life; so to achieve superior results, it is worthwhile to source the best-quality products you can find. Another compelling reason to make your own sweets is to experience the pleasure of eating these desserts, because it's unlikely that there's a master baker in your neighborhood equal to those in Beirut, Tripoli, Istanbul, or Gaziantep. Finally, there's great satisfaction to be had in mastering these intriguing confections.

And with that, I wish you happy sweets making—and eating.

organic eggs, milk, and sugar

I always use organic eggs and milk, mainly because I know that they come from properly raised animals, and also because they taste better. Of course they are more expensive, but the superior results are worth that extra cost. I also specify organic cane sugar in many recipes because it has a more distinct flavor than granulated white sugar. Because it is unrefined, organic cane sugar is golden hued, which slightly affects some dishes, making them a little darker in color, but I don't mind this. However, feel free to use standard white sugar if organic cane sugar is hard to come by where you live or if you are concerned about the cost.

a note about metric measurements

Recipes in this book use both U.S. and metric measurements. When converting U.S. weights and volumes to metric, I have opted to round to an amount that can be easily measured. For example, the exact metric equivalent of 1 ounce is 28.35 grams, but I have made 1 ounce equal to 30 grams. As weights get heavier, I have adjusted my conversions accordingly, and as a result, it is sometimes nearer to the exact weight in ounces. All recipes have been tested using both U.S. and metric measurements.

halva, puddings, and breakfast sweets

moroccan nut halva

SERVES **6**

1²⁄₃ cups [250 g] unbleached all-purpose flour

¾ tsp ground aniseed

2¼ tsp ground cinnamon

4 small grains mastic (optional; see page 55), finely ground in a small mortar with a pestle to yield ¼ tsp powdered mastic

1¼ cups [125 g] sesame seeds

½ cup [80 g] blanched almonds, toasted (see page 25)

Heaping ½ cup [75 g] confectioners' sugar, plus more for sprinkling

⅓ cup [75 g] honey

1½ Tbsp unsalted butter

¼ cup [60 ml] sunflower oil

◆ This healthful confection is prepared during Ramadan, the Muslim month of daytime fasting, and after childbirth as a restorative for the mother.

Put the flour in a frying pan and place over medium heat. Toast the flour, stirring constantly, until it is golden, about 10 minutes—be careful not to let it burn, as it will turn bitter.

Transfer the flour to a large mixing bowl and let cool. Add the aniseed, cinnamon, and mastic (if using) and mix well.

Put the sesame seeds in a small skillet and place over medium heat. Toast the seeds, stirring constantly, until just beginning to change color, about 10 minutes. Let cool.

Process the sesame seeds, ¼ cup [40 g] of the almonds, and the confectioners' sugar in a food processor until very finely ground. Add to the flour and mix well. Make a well in the center.

Heat the honey and butter in a small saucepan but do not let the mixture boil. Add to the well along with the sunflower oil and work together until you have a smooth paste.

Transfer to a shallow serving bowl and shape into a pyramid. Sprinkle with confectioners' sugar and arrange the remaining whole almonds in four lines fanning out from the top of the pyramid and in a line around the bottom. Serve immediately.

halva

Halva made with tahini is well known, but few people know how it's made. And I have to admit I didn't until many years ago, when I prepared it following a published recipe and nearly broke my food processor trying to grind the sesame seeds. I ended up with a halva that bore no resemblance to any I had ever eaten. A few years ago, I was being taken around the old souks of Aleppo by a wonderful character, Hassan Khoja, a burly man with an encyclopedic knowledge of all things Aleppine. We stopped at the shop of a friend of his, Omar Akesh, who sells tahini and halva that he produces in a sprawling and rather medieval space behind and above his shop.

To make tahini, Akesh roasts sesame seeds, and then soaks, hulls, and presses them. He boils soapwort roots to produce a brown liquid that when beaten miraculously turns into a brilliant white foam (because of soapwort's saponin content). He then mixes the foam with sugar syrup to produce a meringue-like dip called *natef* (see page 59). Then the *natef* is mixed with the tahini and the mixture is processed in three different stages. First it is churned in a big metal vat. Next it is beaten with a huge wooden pestle that is attached to an automated arm. After that comes the final stage, kneading: the mixture is transferred to a gorgeous large metal bowl with a round bottom, and the halva maker kneads the mixture as he would dough until it is smooth. He then portions out the halva and packs it in containers.

However, tahini halva is only one type of halva. There are many others, made with semolina or flour, that are prepared for specific occasions. Some cooks start toasting the flour on its own before continuing the browning process with the butter, while others brown the flour and butter together from the very beginning. Some cook the halva with the sugar syrup while others add the syrup away from the heat. And some don't even make any syrup, directly adding confectioners' sugar to the flour to produce a more brittle halva. In any case, flour or semolina halva is a lot easier and quicker to make than tahini halva; and it will keep for a few days, stored in an airtight container kept in a cool place. This kind of halva is basically a spoon sweet. It is either spread in a shallow bowl and then spooned onto individual plates—it has a smooth, creamy texture, a little like dense mashed potatoes—or it is shaped into quenelles for a prettier presentation. I sometimes cut it with tiny cookie cutters.

pumpkin halva

SERVES **8** TO **10**

One 5½-lb [2.5-kg] pumpkin, peeled, seeded, and diced into 1-in [2.5-cm] cubes

4½ cups [1.1 L] water

2⅓ cups [350 g] unbleached all-purpose flour

1½ cups [300 g] organic cane sugar

¾ tsp saffron threads, lightly crushed between your fingers, plus a pinch of whole saffron threads

1½ tsp ground cardamom

2 Tbsp rose water

¼ cup [55 g] ghee, preferably Emirati ghee (see page 14), plus more for garnish

◆ Emirati Arabic is somewhat different from classical Arabic—we classic speakers call pumpkin *qara'*, they call it *boubar*. The food in the Arabian Gulf is also very different from that of Syria, Lebanon, Jordan, and Egypt. This dessert is a perfect example of the sweet-savory desserts that are typical of that part of the Middle East. The recipe was given to me by Umm Sa'id, a marvelous cook who has a huge catering kitchen in al-'Ayn, near Abu Dhabi. I have changed it slightly, using only all-purpose flour and not a combination of all-purpose with a coarser variety not widely available outside the Middle East. You can try replacing the all-purpose flour with fine semolina, but the dessert will be less smooth. You can substitute kabocha or butternut squash for the pumpkin, but do not use the inedible pumpkins used for jack-o'-lanterns. A nice touch is to put small orchids or other flowers in the middle of the platter or on the side if you are plating the dish.

Put the pumpkin in a large saucepan. Add the water and place over medium heat. Bring to a boil, lower the heat, and simmer until the pumpkin softens completely and absorbs most of the water, 25 to 30 minutes.

Meanwhile, put the flour in a large frying pan and toast it over medium heat, stirring constantly, until a nutty aroma rises and it darkens slightly, about 10 minutes. Be sure you don't burn the flour, which will make the halva bitter.

continued

When the pumpkin is ready, mash it in the pan over low heat using a potato masher. Add the sugar and stir until completely dissolved. Add all the saffron and the ground cardamom. Add the rose water and mix well.

Gradually add the toasted flour and combine until you have a smooth mixture. Add the ghee and blend well. Place the lid over the pan and keep warm until ready to serve.

You can serve the halva the traditional way, spread in a shallow bowl and brushed with ghee, or you can make pretty quenelles and arrange these in a rosette on a plate, drizzling them with a little ghee. Serve immediately after plating.

ghee

Ghee (clarified butter) is known as *samneh* or *samna* in Arabic, and it is simply butter that has been stripped of its milk solids. It is a purer fat than butter, so it lasts longer and can be cooked at a higher temperature without burning. Many traditional confectioners use *samneh* but if you prefer to use butter you can, just make sure it is unsalted. You can easily make ghee yourself by heating butter in a saucepan until it starts foaming. Skim the foam, let the milk solids settle on the bottom of the pan, and then carefully pour the clarified butter into a clean jar; you can pour it through cheesecloth if you are finicky. Cover with a lid and store in a cool place or in the refrigerator to use when you need it. Kept covered in the refrigerator, ghee will last for several months. You can substitute olive oil for the butter or ghee. The result will be slightly different, but the recipes will still work. Emirati ghee is the same as any other except that a little turmeric and an Emirati spice mixture called *b'zar* are added to give the ghee a subtle flavor.

chickpea-flour halva

SERVES **4** TO **6**

Pinch of saffron threads

¼ cup [60 ml] rose water

2 cups [250 g] chickpea flour (besan)

1½ tsp ground cardamom

1¼ cups [250 g] organic cane sugar

1 cup [240 ml] boiling water

½ cup [110 g] unsalted butter, melted

2 Tbsp slivered or chopped pistachios

◆ *Khabiss*, a kind of crumbly halva, is a typical hospitality sweet in the Arabian Gulf. It's prepared with semolina or flour, with or without dates. This version is made with chickpea flour, ideal for those who are gluten-intolerant. You can replace the sugar with date syrup for a more intriguing sweet flavor, using 1 cup [240 ml] of date syrup loosened with 3 Tbsp hot water.

In a small bowl, combine the saffron and rose water and set aside to infuse.

Put the chickpea flour in a large frying pan and place over medium heat. Toast, stirring continuously, until the aroma rises, 8 to 10 minutes. You want the color to lighten slightly; be careful not to burn it or it will be bitter. Add the ground cardamom. Mix well and remove from the heat.

Put the sugar in a medium saucepan and place over medium heat. Let the sugar melt, stirring occasionally, and cook until it turns golden, 10 to 15 minutes. As with the flour, be careful not to let the sugar burn. As soon as the sugar is ready, carefully and slowly add the boiling water. It will splatter, so use a long-handled ladle and make sure you keep well away from the pan as you add the water.

Return the chickpea flour to medium heat. Add the melted butter and whisk until well blended. Then add the sugar water and mix well. Turn the heat to the lowest setting and cover the pan. Let steam for about 15 minutes, stirring occasionally. Remove from the heat and add the saffron–rose water mixture.

Transfer the halva to a shallow serving bowl and scatter the pistachios over the top. Serve warm, or within an hour or two of making.

almond pudding

SERVES 4 TO 6

4 cups [960 ml] whole milk

¾ cup [60 g] almond meal

¼ cup [40 g] rice flour or cornstarch

⅓ cup [60 g] organic cane sugar

½ tsp almond extract

1 to 2 Tbsp slivered or chopped pistachios

◆ *Fuqara* means "poor" in Arabic, and I don't know why the word is applied to this pudding. The ingredients aren't particularly associated with poverty, so perhaps this pudding was distributed to the indigent. Who knows? I like to play with the flavor, sometimes replacing the almond extract with the seeds from one vanilla bean, and sometimes I add ground ginger to the almond extract to give the pudding a subtle spicy flavor. Variations like these can be added at the same point in the recipe as the almond extract. You can also make it with almond milk or, if you can find it, use goat's milk instead of the more readily available cow's milk. You can store this pudding, covered with plastic wrap, in the refrigerator for up to 2 days.

Put 3½ cups [840 ml] of the milk in a saucepan over medium heat. Bring to a boil, stirring occasionally—watch it toward the end so as not to let it boil over. As it starts to boil, add the almond meal. Turn the heat to medium-low and let simmer, stirring regularly, until the almond meal has softened and expanded, about 10 minutes.

In a small bowl, mix the rice flour with the remaining ½ cup [120 ml] milk, stirring until completely smooth. Slowly whisk the starch mixture into the simmering milk and cook, whisking all the time, for about 5 minutes until the mixture has thickened.

Add the sugar and continue whisking until completely dissolved. (Taste and adjust the sweetness to your liking, adding a little more sugar if necessary.) Remove from the heat and stir in the almond extract.

Pour the pudding into one large serving bowl or four to six individual bowls, depending on their size. Let cool. Serve at room temperature garnished with the pistachio or refrigerate to serve chilled, reserving the garnish until just before serving.

turkish saffron rice pudding

SERVES **6**

½ tsp saffron threads

2 Tbsp rose water

Heaping ½ cup [110 g] Calasparra rice or other short-grain rice

¾ cup plus 2 Tbsp [175 g] superfine sugar

1 Tbsp slivered almonds

1 Tbsp slivered or chopped pistachios, plus more for garnish

Pomegranate seeds for garnish (optional)

◆ Rice pudding is common across the Middle East and North Africa, with each country having its own variation. The Lebanese, Syrians, Egyptians, and Moroccans prepare it with milk, while the Turks and Iranians have a less creamy but equally luxurious version served at weddings and circumcisions that is flavored with saffron, the world's most expensive spice. In Turkey, the pudding is called *zerde*, from the Persian *shol-e zard*, and unlike the others, it is made with just water. Here, you can use either short-grain rice for a more mushy texture that resembles congee, or the superior Calasparra (paella) rice, which retains its shape even when cooked for a long time. Made with the latter, your pudding will have more texture, with the grains remaining separate even when very soft. You can store the ungarnished rice pudding, covered with plastic wrap, in the refrigerator for up to 2 days; bring to room temperature before serving.

Put the saffron threads to soak in the rose water.

Rinse the rice under cold water to get rid of some of the starch and put in a saucepan. Add 5 cups [1.2 L] water and place over medium heat. Bring to a boil. Add the sugar. Turn the heat to low and let simmer for about 30 minutes, or until the rice has expanded and is very soft.

Add the nuts, saffron–rose water mixture, and another ¼ cup [60 ml] water. Simmer for another 5 minutes. The rice should be like a thin porridge; it will thicken as it sits. Divide equally among six individual bowls or pour into one large serving bowl. Let cool to serve at room temperature, garnished with more pistachios and pomegranate seeds, if desired.

HALVA, PUDDINGS, AND BREAKFAST SWEETS

spices

Spices are used quite regularly in both Middle Eastern and North African sweets. Aniseed, the seeds from a flowering plant in the fennel family, is native to the eastern Mediterranean and southwestern Asia. Tasting of licorice, aniseed is used in both seed and ground form to flavor desserts.

Caraway seed is also used as a dessert flavoring. It is known as Persian cumin, probably because it resembles cumin, but it tastes a little like anise.

Cardamom (*hal* in Arabic) is native to India, Nepal, and Bhutan. A member of the ginger family, it is obtained from several plants of the similar genera *Elettaria* and *Amomum*. It is the second-most expensive spice in the world, after saffron. In Lebanon, cardamom is mostly used in Turkish coffee, whereas in other parts of the Arab world, and especially in the Arabian Gulf, it has wider culinary applications. I prefer to use green cardamom pods, which are basically the fresher version of the pale ones. Neither should be confused with black cardamom, which is actually not cardamom but a close relative.

Cinnamon (*qerfa* in Arabic) is obtained from two different types of cinnamon tree, both from the laurel family. The thin sheets of the inner part of the bark of *Cinnamomum zeylanicum* are dried and rolled into thin quills to produce "real" stick cinnamon. These are sold in the West, usually cut to the same short length, whereas in Lebanon and elsewhere in the Middle East they are left uncut and can be found measuring as long as 12 in [30.5 cm]. The thick, dark bark of *Cinnamomum cassia* is known as cassia and is the variety chiefly used in the Middle East because of its strong flavor.

Saffron (*za'faran* in Arabic) is the most expensive spice in the world, obtained from the stigmas of the crocus flower, which are picked by hand. Because each flower has only three stigmas, masses of flowers have to be picked to produce a few grams of saffron. Saffron is used extensively in Iran and the Arabian Gulf but less so in Lebanon, Syria, and Turkey. Its quality varies, with the costliest saffron grown in Kashmir. As long as the stigmas are not mixed with anything else, any variety will be fine. Beware the fake saffron that is sold cheaply in souks; it is safflower, and all it will do is give you a yellow color but no flavor. And worse than safflower is the totally fake saffron made up of colored threads that color water red instead of yellow. Iranians and Gulf Arabs soak the threads in water or rose water before using them. Iranians also crush the saffron first, which makes it easier to measure. I prefer to use the threads whole, as I love seeing them scattered inside puddings or other desserts. The flavor is also more intense in the bite that has the thread in it, because the saffron continues to bleed into the pudding.

Mahlab is a spice ground from the kernel of a black cherry (*Prunus mahaleb*), native to Asia Minor. You can buy *mahlab* whole or ground to use in cookies. The flavor is pronounced, nutty with a hint of bitterness, and a little goes a long way.

sago pudding with almonds and pistachios

SERVES **6**

1 cup [175 g] small sago pearls (see facing page)

¼ tsp saffron threads

2 Tbsp rose water

1 cup [200 g] organic cane sugar

2 Tbsp sunflower oil

1½ tsp ground cardamom

Ghee (see page 14), for brushing (optional)

¼ cup [40 g] slivered almonds

¼ cup [40 g] slivered or chopped pistachios

◆ The first time I tasted this pudding was at the Heritage House in Sharjah, one of the seven United Arab Emirates, where my friend Sheikha Bodour al-Qasimi introduced me to Emirati food. She had arranged for the ladies who cook at the center to show me how to prepare an incredible selection of sumptuous Emirati dishes for us to feast on. When it came time for dessert, I uncovered a large dish and found *sago*. I loved the translucent orange color and the little bubbles all over but didn't know anything about it because the ladies had brought it with them. Sheikha Bodour explained that it was one of their classic desserts, made with tiny sago pellets and caramelized sugar and flavored with saffron and cardamom, the two most expensive spices in the world. When it came to helping myself I struggled to get just a little on the spoon—it seemed to stretch almost indefinitely. Luckily, one of the ladies had no trouble scooping a large portion onto my plate, which I ate with pleasure. Both the texture—half jelly, half thick pudding—and the subtle, not-too-sweet flavor enhanced by the spices were tantalizing. Sago is really best eaten on the day it is prepared, served warm or at room temperature.

Soak the sago pearls in 1 cup [240 ml] water for 1 hour. Soak the saffron in the rose water.

Bring 4 cups [460 ml] water to a boil.

Put the sugar in a saucepan and place over medium heat. Stir the sugar until it has completely melted and is golden brown, 8 to 10 minutes, being careful not to let it burn. Carefully add the boiling water a little at a time—the water will splatter as soon as it touches the caramel, so cover your hand and arm and turn your face away. Let bubble until the caramel has completely dissolved in the water.

Add the sago to the caramel syrup. Let it simmer, stirring very regularly, until the sago has swelled and you no longer see any trails of white, about 30 minutes. The mixture should be sticky but not too thick, a little like stretchy jelly.

Add the sunflower oil and cardamom and mix well. Add the saffron–rose water mixture and combine well. Remove from the heat and pour into a shallow 1½-qt [1.5-L] serving bowl. Let cool a little, and then brush the surface with ghee. Once the pudding has cooled to room temperature, scatter the nuts all over and serve.

sago

Sago pearls are tiny white pellets of starch extracted from the pith of the trunk of a sago palm or similar species of palm. Sago can also be extracted from the trunk of some cycads. To get the sago, the ten- to fifteen-year-old palms are chopped down just before they flower; the trunk is cut into sections to facilitate the extraction of its heart. The starch is then separated and made into a dough that is pressed through a sieve to produce pearls of different sizes. Those used in the Sago Pudding with Almonds and Pistachios are small, more or less the size of brown lentils. Even though sago is similar to tapioca when cooked, it is not the same starch. Sago, on its own, does not have much flavor; its appeal lies in the texture that it brings to the dish.

egyptian bread pudding

SERVES **4** TO **6**

5 Tbsp [50 g] raisins

9 oz [250 g] *marquq* (hand-kerchief bread) or thin lavash

2⅓ cups [350 g] mixed nuts (such as pistachios, hazel-nuts, peanuts, cashews, almonds, and walnuts)

3 cups [720 ml] whole milk

½ cup [100 g] organic cane sugar

1 Tbsp orange blossom water

Crème fraîche for serving

◆ *Umm 'ali* is the classic Egyptian dessert, an Arab version of bread pudding made with layers of very thin, crisp flat bread soaked with sweetened milk and topped with nuts. Egyptians sprinkle the bread with a little melted butter. I skip this step for a lighter dessert. I also use a larger quantity of nuts for more crunch. And finally, I add a little orange blossom water to the milk to lift the flavor. Egyptians use a flat bread called *reqaq* (meaning flattened very thin), which is not widely available, so I use *marquq* (handkerchief bread) or the thinnest lavash I can find, and toast the bread in the oven before using. It works very well, though I find it somewhat counterintuitive to crisp bread and then soak it immediately in milk; but if you serve *umm 'ali* straight out of the oven, the bread will retain a little crunch. In fact, you really need to time your dessert so that you serve it immediately out of the oven. You can reheat leftovers, but add a little milk or cream before serving.

In a small bowl, cover the raisins with water and let soak at room temperature for about 1 hour, until plump and softened.

Preheat the oven to 400°F [200°C].

Lay one sheet of *marquq* on a large baking sheet and toast in the oven until crisp and golden, about 8 minutes. Remove from the oven and repeat with the remaining *marquq*. Maintain the oven temperature.

Break the toasted bread into medium-size pieces and arrange in an oval baking dish measuring about 11 by 6 in [28 by 25 cm] with sides about 2½ in [6 cm] high.

Spread the nuts on a large baking sheet and place in the oven. Toast until golden brown, 10 to 12 minutes. Remove from the oven and let cool; maintain the oven temperature.

Put the milk and sugar in a saucepan and place over medium heat. Bring to a boil, stirring every now and then. Remove from the heat and add the orange blossom water.

Pour the hot milk over the bread. Drain the raisins and sprinkle them along with the nuts all over the bread.

Bake until the milk is almost completely absorbed and the bread is a little crisp around the edges, about 20 minutes. Serve immediately, dolloped with crème fraîche.

preparing nuts

In the old days, I toasted my nuts in a little butter in a pan on the stove top, stirring them all the time until they colored, but now I spread them on a baking sheet and toast them in a 400°F [200°C] oven for anything between 6 and 9 minutes, depending on what nut I am using, until the nuts are golden brown and crisp. They color just as evenly and I save time and extra fat.

Sometimes my recipes specify soaking the nuts. This is to make them easy to peel if that is a step you choose to take, but more important, the soaking rehydrates them and makes them taste as if they were fresh from the tree. I soak them overnight in enough water to cover them in the bowl. This step will not, however, restore rancid nuts, which should be thrown out.

turkish sweet chicken pudding

SERVES **4** TO **6**

3 oz [90 g] boneless, skinless chicken breast

3 cups [720 ml] whole milk

½ cup [75 g] rice flour

⅓ cup [65 g] organic cane sugar, or to taste

Orange Blossom Jam (page 128) or ground cinnamon for garnish

◆ This unusual dessert is a classic in Turkey. Western tastes and conventions find a dessert made with chicken a little eccentric. You can't taste the chicken, but it adds a thick, stretchy texture to this not-so-sweet dish. The dish can be prepared two ways; the first is plain, as in the basic instructions that follow. For the other version, the mixture is poured into a skillet and caramelized on one side. You can then either cut it into squares and serve them caramelized-side up, or roll it up showing the caramelized side and serve like a jelly roll. I like the caramelized version, but at home it is easier to prepare it plain. For the adventurous, I also give instructions for the caramelized variation.

Put the chicken in a small saucepan, add enough water to cover, and place over medium heat. Bring to a boil; lower the heat and simmer for 30 minutes, or until very tender. Remove the chicken and rinse under cold water; shred into fine threads. (The threads should mostly disappear into the pudding, with only the occasional bite containing a discernible bit of chicken.) Rinse again and pat dry with paper towels. Cover and set aside.

Bring 2 cups [480 ml] of the milk to a boil over medium-high heat. Mix the remaining 1 cup [240 ml] milk with the rice flour, stirring until creamy. Turn the heat under the milk to low and whisk the rice flour mixture into the hot milk. Keep whisking for 10 minutes. Add the sugar and cook for another 10 minutes, whisking all the time. Stir in the shredded chicken and continue cooking, whisking all the time, for another 10 minutes or so. You want the chicken to disappear almost completely in the pudding.

Divide the mixture equally among four or six individual bowls, or pour it into one large serving dish. Let cool, and then refrigerate for about 2 hours to serve chilled, either topped with a spoonful of the jam or sprinkled with a little cinnamon.

Variation: To make the caramelized version, after the whisking stage, pour the pudding into a medium-size rectangular nonstick baking pan to a thickness of about ¾ in [1.5 cm]. Place one corner of the pan over very low heat and let the bottom caramelize for 10 to 15 minutes, until it turns dark brown. Turn the dish to let another corner caramelize. Continue turning the dish until the entire bottom has browned. (You could use a round pan, which will make it easier and quicker—only 10 to 15 minutes total—to brown the bottom evenly because you heat the entire pan at once; however, because of the round edges, you won't be able to cut the entire pudding into rectangles.) Once the bottom has browned, cut the pudding into about six rectangles, lifting each off the pan and rolling as you go along to serve like a jelly roll. Cover and refrigerate for about 2 hours until chilled, or for up to 1 day, before serving.

bread of
the seraglio

SERVES **4** TO **6**

One day-old 8-in [20-cm] round loaf of bread

1¼ cups [250 g] organic cane sugar

1 tsp freshly squeezed lemon juice

1 tsp orange blossom water

1 Tbsp rose water

1¼ cups [300 g] Middle Eastern Clotted Cream (page 31) or English clotted cream

2 Tbsp coarsely chopped unsalted pistachios

◆ Depending on how you read *seraglio* (the word means both "harem" and "sultan's palace"), this dish of Turkish origin could be an inexpensive dessert served to concubines or one fit for kings. But if the latter, then why the modest basic ingredient of stale bread? Either way, no Arab would view *'aysh al-saraya* as anything but a luxurious dessert with lavish amounts of clotted cream covering a bread base soaked in caramelized sugar syrup. It is often eaten alone as a sweet treat either at the confectioner's or at home, or served as a dessert at the end of a special meal. The soft textures and different temperatures (chilled clotted cream on top of warm bread when served immediately after preparing) are heavenly, and I always find it very difficult to resist a second helping.

Trim off and discard the crust of the bread, or reserve it for making bread crumbs. Tear the bread into irregular 1-in [2.5-cm] pieces.

In a medium saucepan, combine 3 Tbsp water, the sugar, and lemon juice. Bring to a boil over medium heat and cook, stirring constantly so that the sugar does not recrystallize, until the syrup has caramelized to a golden brown color, about 15 minutes; be careful not to burn it.

continued

Put some water to boil and measure out ¾ cup [180 ml]. Gradually add the boiling water to the syrup, stirring with a long-handled wooden spoon; the syrup will splatter when you add the water, so make sure you do this very slowly and cautiously. Remove from the heat and add the orange blossom water and rose water.

Add the bread to the syrup and cook over medium heat for 5 to 10 minutes, pressing down and mashing the bread with the back of the spoon to help it soak up the syrup. The bread should absorb the syrup and become quite mushy.

Spread the bread in an even layer on an 8-in [20-cm] round serving platter. If there is any syrup left in the pan, pour it over the bread. Let cool for about 20 minutes.

Spread the clotted cream over the bread, leaving a little of the edge showing, and either garnish with the pistachios to serve immediately or cover and refrigerate for up to 1 day to serve later, in which case garnish just before serving it chilled.

middle eastern clotted cream

MAKES 1¾ CUPS [420 ML]

1⅓ cups [320 ml] whole milk
⅓ cup [50 g] fine semolina
¼ cup [60 ml] heavy cream

◆ Years ago, I was wandering through Tripoli in northern Lebanon, hoping to come across interesting street food. Instead, I struck gold when I peeked through a doorway to find a group of men making *qashta*, the Arab version of English clotted cream. They were skimming cream off milk that was bubbling in huge shallow, round pans set over gas burners; the skimmed cream was left to drain before being packed into containers. The vast room in which they worked was dark except for shafts of sunlight streaming through the narrow windows, and the scene was rather medieval. But I was brought back to the modern world when they told me they were using powdered milk to make the *qashta*. The magic of the moment was broken.

Fortunately, not all *qashta* is made with powdered milk. Some use sheep's milk, which produces the most luxurious *qashta*. I occasionally make the cream at home using fresh milk that I let simmer on the corner of the stove, but I more often rely on this much faster method, which thickens the milk with semolina and cream. You can also use cornstarch or white bread crumbs. The result is not the same as with the slow method, which requires a large quantity of milk that yields only a small amount of cream, but it's much quicker to make, and even professionals are using this method now.

In Turkey, *kaymak* is served for breakfast; in Lebanon and Syria, it's served both as a dessert, drizzled with honey, and as a filling or garnish for pastry.

Put the milk in a saucepan and stir in the semolina and cream. Place over medium-low heat and bring to a boil, whisking constantly to avoid lumps. Boil for another 3 to 5 minutes, continuing to whisk, until the mixture is thicker than crème fraîche or sour cream. Let cool. Store in an airtight container in the refrigerator for up to 3 days.

date "granola"

MAKES ABOUT **3** CUPS [**500** G]

1½ cups [225 g] whole-wheat flour

1 tsp ground cardamom, plus more for sprinkling

½ tsp ground ginger

1½ cups [225 g] pitted soft dates, coarsely chopped

¼ cup [55 g] ghee (see page 14) or unsalted butter, melted

½ cup [60 g] walnuts, blanched almonds, or a mixture, toasted (see page 25) and coarsely chopped

◆ I discovered this softly crumbly sweet in the United Arab Emirates. It is one of their classic confections, normally served for breakfast with such other typical breakfast dishes as *balalit*, a sweet-savory noodle dish, and *l'geimat*, saffron-scented fritters (see page 40). I have had *bathith* served as a crumbly mixture in a bowl, to be eaten with fingers or a spoon, and I have had it pressed into shapes in *ma'mul* molds (see page 56), which made for a prettier presentation. Even though *bathith* is not at all like granola (it has a softer texture), I like to think of it as the Arabian version, in which whole-wheat flour replaces oats and dates replace raisins; it looks and tastes just as wholesome as granola. The Deglet Noor variety of dates works well.

This recipe is adapted from one I found in *A Taste of the Arabian Gulf*, a lovely book on Gulf cooking written by Afnan Rashid al-Zayani.

In a large skillet, toast the flour over medium heat, stirring constantly, until it releases a nutty aroma and darkens slightly, 8 to 10 minutes. Take care not to burn the flour or it will taste bitter. Transfer the flour to a large mixing bowl. Add the 1 tsp cardamom and the ginger and mix well.

Add the dates and ghee and stir until you have a crumbly mixture. Stir in the nuts and transfer to a serving bowl. Sprinkle with a little ground cardamom. Store in an airtight container, in a cool place (not the refrigerator), for up to 2 weeks.

Variation: You can make *bathith* less spicy by omitting the ground ginger, or for a different, though unorthodox, flavor, you can use cinnamon and allspice instead of cardamom and ginger. If you want to mold it, reduce the amount of flour by ¾ cup [115 g]; pinch off small amounts of *bathith*, roll into balls, and gently press inside the mold. Tap out the molded *bathith* and place on a serving platter. You can make it sweeter by drizzling with date syrup just before serving.

sweet couscous with almonds and cinnamon

SERVES **6** TO **8**

2½ cups [500 g] fine couscous (not precooked)

1 tsp fine sea salt

1 Tbsp extra-virgin olive oil

6 Tbsp [85 g] unsalted butter; 2 Tbsp melted, 4 Tbsp [55 g] at room temperature

1 cup [150 g] blanched almonds

3 Tbsp confectioners' sugar, plus more for sprinkling

Ground cinnamon for garnish

◆ Moroccans enjoy a course called *avant les desserts* (before the desserts) that includes this sweet couscous. It is served at the end of the meal, not so much as a dessert but as a semi-sweet finish before the fruit and mint tea arrive. I prefer to have it for breakfast, even if none of my Moroccan friends approves. *Seffa* is normally prepared with the finest-grade couscous, which is not precooked like most grocery-store varieties. In fact, hardly anyone in Morocco uses precooked couscous—that is, the type you pour boiling water over and let sit until the liquid is absorbed.

Moroccans like their couscous very fluffy, and the only way to achieve that is to use regular couscous and steam it at least twice. Many cooks steam it up to five times. I am with the Moroccans on this, so I buy my couscous from specialty shops and steam it. Soaking precooked couscous may be a lot quicker, but the texture is never as good as steamed; and in the case of *seffa*, the difference is even more noticeable.

Put the couscous in a shallow mixing bowl.

Dissolve the salt in ⅔ cup [160 ml] water. Sprinkle the salted water over the couscous little by little, stirring the grain with your fingers as you go along to wet the couscous evenly and break up any lumps. When the couscous has soaked up all the water, stir in the olive oil.

Fill a pot into which you can insert a steamer one-quarter full with water. (Use a *couscoussière* if you have one.) If the holes of your steamer are so large that the couscous will fall through, line it with cheesecloth. Put the couscous in the top part of your steamer and set over the pot of water. Ideally, no steam should escape from the joint between the pan and the steamer, so if necessary, wrap a strip of cloth around the edge of the pot before slotting in the steamer. Place over medium-high heat and, when the water comes to a boil, steam the couscous, covered, for 20 minutes.

Tip the couscous into a bowl and sprinkle, again little by little, with another ⅔ cup [160 ml] water, this time using a wooden spoon to stir and break up the lumps as the grain will be too hot for your hand—most Moroccan cooks use their hands, which seem to be made of asbestos! Add the melted butter and stir well. Let sit, covered with a clean kitchen towel, for 15 minutes to fluff up.

Preheat the oven to 450°F [220°C].

Return the couscous to the top part of the steamer and set over the pan of boiling water. Steam, uncovered, for another 15 minutes.

While the couscous is steaming, spread the almonds over a baking sheet and toast in the oven until golden brown, 7 or 8 minutes. Remove from the oven and let cool before coarsely grinding two-thirds of the almonds in a food processor. (The remaining whole almonds will be used for a garnish.)

Add the room-temperature butter and confectioners' sugar to the hot couscous and mix well. Tip half of the couscous into a medium-size shallow serving bowl and spread the ground almonds evenly over it. Sprinkle with a little more confectioners' sugar and cover with the remaining couscous. Using the back of a spoon, arrange the couscous in a mound with a pointed top. Sprinkle ground cinnamon lightly in four thin lines fanning out from the top to the bottom. Line up the whole almonds between the lines of cinnamon. Serve hot, with more confectioners' sugar and cinnamon for those who like them.

wheat berry and nut porridge with aniseed

SERVES **6**

- ⅔ cup [100 g] blanched almonds
- ⅔ cup [100 g] walnuts
- ⅓ cup [50 g] pine nuts
- 1¼ cups [250 g] hulled wheat berries
- 1½ tsp ground aniseed
- 1 cup [200 g] organic cane sugar
- 2 Tbsp orange blossom water
- 2 Tbsp rose water

◆ *Sinn* means "teeth" in Arabic, and *snayniye* is prepared to celebrate babies' first teeth and the beginning of their ability to eat proper food. The porridge is not given to the baby but is offered to friends and family coming to congratulate the proud parents, or it is sent away to loved ones and neighbors to celebrate the good news. I use hulled wheat here, but you can also use barley. The soft, chewy texture of the cooked wheat offers a lovely contrast to the fresh crunch of the soaked nuts, the whole enhanced by the fragrant waters. This delightful sweet snack also makes a delectable breakfast. It is prepared by Christians on December 4 to commemorate Saint Barbara, an early saint and martyr. Make sure to start soaking the nuts the night before you want to make this.

Place the almonds, walnuts, and pine nuts in three separate small bowls and pour in enough water to cover. Let soak overnight. If you have the patience, peel the soaked walnuts, discarding the skins.

Rinse the wheat berries and put them in a large saucepan. Add 1 qt [960 ml] water and place over medium heat. Bring to a boil; lower the heat and let simmer for 1 hour, or until the wheat berries are completely tender and have opened up a little. The cooking water should be a thick broth.

Add the ground aniseed, sugar, orange blossom water, and rose water and stir until the sugar has dissolved.

Drain and rinse the nuts, keeping them separate. Divide the wheat berries among six individual bowls. Scatter the nuts over the top and serve hot, warm, or at room temperature.

fritters, pancakes, and pastries

fritters in saffron syrup

MAKES **25** TO **30** FRITTERS

syrup

2 cups [400 g] organic cane sugar

Pinch of ground cardamom

1 small cinnamon stick

Pinch of saffron threads

1 Tbsp freshly squeezed lemon juice

1 cup [240 ml] water

fritters

2 cups [300 g] unbleached all-purpose flour

Heaping 1 tsp fast-acting (instant) yeast

¼ tsp fine sea salt

1 Tbsp organic cane sugar

½ cup [120 ml] whole-milk yogurt

½ cup [120 ml] water

1 large egg

Sunflower oil for frying

◆ I don't often fry at home, but I make an exception for these fragrant fritters. This ancient Arab sweet is traditionally drizzled with date syrup and is found, under different names, across the Middle East. The crunchy Lebanese version I grew up with is called *'uwwamat* and is dipped in sugar syrup flavored with rose water and orange blossom water (see page 46). Some cooks in the Gulf dip them in sugar syrup flavored with cardamom, cinnamon, and saffron; that is the version I offer here. Both are heavenly combinations.

To make the syrup: Put the sugar, cardamom, cinnamon, saffron, lemon juice, and water in a saucepan. Place over low heat. Simmer for about 15 minutes, stirring every now and then, until you have a thick syrup. Remove from the heat and set aside.

To make the fritters: Mix the flour, yeast, salt, and sugar in a large mixing bowl. Add the yogurt, water, and egg; stir until you have a very loose dough or a very thick batter. Cover with plastic wrap and let rest for at least 3 hours, or up to overnight, at cool room temperature.

Pour enough sunflower oil into a large, deep frying pan to reach a depth of 2 in [5 cm]. Place over medium heat. Check the temperature by dropping a little dough into the oil; if the oil bubbles around it, it's ready. (A candy thermometer should register 350°F [180°C].) There are several traditional ways of dropping the dough into the hot oil. One is to wet your hands and with the tips of your fingers pinch off enough dough to make a ball the size of an apricot. Another method is to grab a small handful of the dough, make a fist, and squeeze the dough between your thumb and index finger to create a ball of dough about the size of a walnut. Using a wet spoon, scoop up the ball of dough. An easier way to do this, though it's not traditional, is to wet an ice-cream scoop and use that to form the fritters. Drop as many fritters into the hot oil as will fit comfortably without overcrowding.

Fry the fritters until golden brown all over, stirring them regularly so that they color evenly, about 10 minutes. Using a slotted spoon, transfer to a wire rack set over a plate and let the excess oil drain off. Repeat with the remaining dough, making sure the oil does not get too hot.

Drop the drained fritters into the syrup. Stir a few times and then, using a slotted spoon, transfer the fritters to a shallow bowl. Serve immediately.

ZALABIA

spiced finger fritters

MAKES ABOUT **26** FRITTERS

- **1⅔ cups [250 g] unbleached all-purpose flour**
- **1 Tbsp ground aniseed**
- **½ tsp ground cinnamon**
- **1 tsp fast-acting (instant) yeast**
- **2 Tbsp extra-virgin olive oil**
- **½ cup [100 g] superfine sugar**
- **½ cup plus 2 Tbsp [150 ml] whole milk**
- **Sunflower oil for frying**

◆ *Zalabia* are a specialty of the mountains, and one of the very few sweets that are exclusively homemade. Christians prepare them for Epiphany (Ghtass) while Muslims make them during Ramadan, the month of fast. The name can be confusing, as it means different things in different countries. In Iran, for instance, *zalabia* describes syrupy braided fritters, which are known as *mushabbak* in Lebanon. I prefer this version, which is not so sweet. When served immediately after frying, the fritters have an appealing soft crunch. I also love the aniseed flavor, which always takes me back to our summers in the mountains, when my grandmother made them to welcome us the day we arrived from Beirut. Some people sprinkle *zalabia* with a little confectioners' or granulated sugar before serving, but I find they are sweet enough without any additional sugar.

Mix the flour, ground aniseed, cinnamon, and yeast in a mixing bowl and make a well in the center. Pour the olive oil into the well and rub it into the flour with your fingers until completely incorporated.

Stir the sugar into the milk until dissolved; add to the flour. Mix with a spatula until you have a loose dough. Cover with a damp, not sopping, towel and let sit for 1 hour, until risen.

Pour enough sunflower oil into a large, deep frying pan to reach a depth of 2 in [5 cm]. Place over medium heat. Check the temperature by dropping a little piece of dough into the oil; if the oil bubbles around it, it's ready. (A candy thermometer should register 350°F [180°C].) Moisten your fingers and pinch off a knob of dough the size of a large apricot. Stretch the dough into a long fingerlike shape, about 4 to 6 in [10 to 15 cm] long by 1¼ in [3 cm] wide. Drop as many fritters into the oil as will fit comfortably without overcrowding.

Fry until golden brown all over, stirring them regularly so that they color evenly, 2 to 3 minutes on each side. The dough will puff up during frying and the fritters will end up looking like round, golden alien growths out of a science-fiction film (ideal for children's parties). Using a slotted spoon, transfer to a wire rack. Set over a plate and let the excess oil drain off. Repeat with the remaining dough fingers, making sure the oil does not get too hot. Serve at room temperature.

turkish fritters

MAKES ABOUT **24** FRITTERS

1½ cups [360 ml] Fragrant Sugar Syrup (recipe follows)

½ vanilla bean, split lengthwise

fritters

⅓ cup [80 ml] whole milk

6 Tbsp [85 g] unsalted butter

½ cup [120 ml] water

1 cup [150 g] unbleached all-purpose flour

1 Tbsp semolina (regular, not fine)

½ tsp fine sea salt

1 Tbsp arrowroot

3 large eggs

Sunflower oil for frying

◆ These Turkish fritters, sold on the street, are similar to the Spanish churros except that they are traditionally made in rings. You can choose to make them immensely sweet by immersing them in the syrup for a while, as some do in Turkey, or you can have them moderately sweet and scrumptiously crunchy if you dip them in the syrup for only a few minutes, as directed. The sugar syrup used here is in the Lebanese and Syrian style, with rose water and orange blossom water, except that I have added half of a vanilla bean. In Iran only rose water is used, while in Turkey they often like their sugar syrup without any flavorings. In Gulf countries it is flavored with saffron and cardamom. In Morocco, heated honey is used instead of syrup.

Heat the sugar syrup in a saucepan over medium heat and add the vanilla bean. Let the vanilla infuse the syrup while cooling.

To make the fritters: Put the milk, butter, and water in a saucepan; place over medium heat and bring to a boil. Stir the flour, semolina, salt, and arrowroot together in a mixing bowl and add to the milk mixture as soon as it comes to a boil. Remove from the heat and stir quickly and vigorously until you have a smooth paste. Return the pan to low heat and cook, stirring all the time, for a couple of minutes. Transfer to a mixing bowl. Cover with a clean kitchen towel and let cool for about 10 minutes.

Add the eggs, one by one, whisking until each is completely incorporated. The mixture will soften and become glossy. Spoon it into a pastry bag fitted with a medium star-shape tip.

continued

Pour enough sunflower oil into a large, deep frying pan to reach a depth of 1½ to 2 in [4 to 5 cm]. Place over medium heat. Check the temperature by dropping a little batter into the oil; if the oil bubbles around it, it's ready. (A candy thermometer should register 350°F [180°C].) Pipe the fritters in 2-in [5-cm] sections directly into the hot oil. You can also pipe them out in rings as they do on the streets of Turkey.

Fry, turning them so that they color evenly, for a few minutes on each side, until they turn a deep brown.

Remove the fritters using a slotted spoon and drop them into the cooled syrup. Let them soak in the syrup for a few minutes, and then transfer to a serving dish. Repeat the process, making sure the oil doesn't get too hot. The fritters are best served immediately or soon after frying, but you can store them in an air-tight container at room temperature for up to 1 day. They will soften but will still be good.

fragrant sugar syrup

MAKES ABOUT 1½ CUPS [360 ML]

2 cups [400 g] superfine sugar

1½ tsp freshly squeezed lemon juice

½ cup [120 ml] water

1 Tbsp rose water

1 Tbsp orange blossom water

Put the sugar, lemon juice, and water in a saucepan and place over medium heat. Bring to a boil, stirring occasionally to help the sugar dissolve. Boil for 3 minutes, and then add the rose water and orange blossom water. Mix well and remove from the heat. Let cool before using unless the recipe instructs otherwise. Store in the refrigerator for up to 2 weeks. Bring to room temperature before using.

moroccan pancakes

MAKES ABOUT **6** PANCAKES

1⅓ cups [200 g] fine semolina

⅓ cup [50 g] unbleached all-purpose flour

1 tsp fast-acting (instant) yeast

½ tsp fine sea salt

1 large egg

1¾ cups [420 ml] whole milk

Sunflower oil for frying

Unsalted butter for serving

Honey for serving

◆ Whereas American pancakes are soft and fluffy, these are soft and chewy—basically a larger, thinner version of English muffins, though made with milk. For a lighter version, you can replace ¾ cup [180 ml] of the milk with water. In Morocco, the pancakes are sold on the street as a morning snack or made at home, usually for breakfast, served with butter and honey. I often replace the butter with thick yogurt. They reheat well, so you can easily prepare them the night before and keep them covered until the morning to reheat in a medium oven before serving. They also freeze well; all you have to do is put them frozen into a hot oven to defrost and heat in one go.

Mix the semolina, flour, yeast, and salt in a large mixing bowl. Beat the egg and stir it into the milk. Gradually add the milk mixture to the semolina and whisk for about 10 minutes, until you have a creamy batter. Cover with plastic wrap and let sit in a warm place for 2 hours.

When the batter is bubbly, lightly oil a nonstick frying pan and place over medium heat. When the pan is hot, pour in a ladleful of batter to make a pancake measuring 7 to 8 in [18 to 20 cm] in diameter. Cook on one side for 2 minutes, or until the top has become completely pockmarked and dry. The pancake will be smooth and golden on the cooked side. Transfer to a clean kitchen towel and finish making the rest of the pancakes. Oil the pan again after making the second pancake and again after the fourth. Don't pile the pancakes on top of each other until they have cooled completely. You can make these smaller by dropping into the pan by the tablespoonful. Serve the pancakes with butter and honey.

FRITTERS, PANCAKES, AND PASTRIES

•47•

walnut pancakes

MAKES **12** SMALL PANCAKES

¾ cup [110 g] unbleached all-purpose flour

½ tsp fast-acting (instant) yeast

Pinch of fine sea salt

½ cup plus 2 Tbsp [150 ml] water

walnut filling

Scant 2 cups [200 g] walnuts

1 Tbsp granulated sugar

¼ tsp ground cinnamon

1 Tbsp orange blossom water

Sunflower oil for frying

Fragrant Sugar Syrup (page 46)

◆ Before the uprising in Syria, I visited the country often, both on my own and to lead culinary tours. In the souks of Damascus, and in particular in Souk Madhat Pasha, I went to my special friends, the Ramadan brothers, who make the best pancakes I've ever eaten on the street. Lebanese/Syrian pancakes are smooth on one side and pockmarked on the other, a little like English muffins. They come in two sizes: a dainty 2 in [1 cm] wide or a regular 4 in [10 cm]. I loved watching the young men at the Ramadan brothers' stall make *qatayef*; how they stirred the batter by hand, poured it into a funny kind of funneled implement before pouring it in spurts onto the hot griddle. While one made the pancakes, another filled them with cheese, walnuts, or clotted cream; fried them; and then dropped them into a large pot of sugar syrup. I always asked them to fry mine on the spot. *Qatayef* are at their crunchy best eaten immediately after frying.

Mix the flour, yeast, and salt in a mixing bowl. Add the water and whisk until you have a smooth batter. Cover with plastic wrap and let sit for 1 hour, until the batter has about doubled and its surface is quite bubbly.

To make the walnut filling: In a food processor, grind the walnuts until medium fine; you want the nuts to retain some texture. In a medium mixing bowl, combine the walnuts, sugar, cinnamon, and orange blossom water.

Shortly before the batter is ready, grease a shallow frying pan with a little sunflower oil and place it over medium heat. When the pan is very hot, measure out a heaped 1 Tbsp of batter and pour it into the pan, to create a disk about 2¾ in [7 cm] in diameter and ¼ in [6 mm] thick. It is best to spread the batter with the back of the spoon as you are pouring it into the pan because it will be too thick to spread by tilting the pan. Cook on one side for 2 to 3 minutes, or until the bottom is lightly browned and the top is bubbly and dry. Transfer to a clean kitchen towel and finish making the rest in the same way. Let the pancakes cool.

One at a time, lay a pancake on your hand, smooth-side down. Spread 1 Tbsp of walnut filling in a line down the middle, leaving the edges clear. Fold the pancake in half, aligning the edges; using your fingers, pinch the edges tightly shut together—you do not want them to open during frying. Place each filled pancake on the kitchen towel and continue filling the rest.

Pour enough sunflower oil into a large, deep frying pan to reach a depth of 2 in [5 cm]. Place over medium heat. Check the temperature by dipping the corner of a pancake into the oil; if the oil bubbles around it, it's ready. A candy thermometer should register 350°F [180°C]. Slide in as many pancakes into the pan as will fit comfortably without crowding.

Fry the pancakes until golden brown all over, 2 to 3 minutes on each side.

Remove the pancakes using a slotted spoon and drop them into the sugar syrup. Turn in the syrup until well coated, and then transfer to a serving dish. Repeat the process. The pancakes are best served immediately, or no more than an hour after you have fried them; otherwise they may soften.

crispy algerian "crêpes"

MAKES **12** "CRÊPES"

2⅔ cups [300 g] semolina (regular, not fine)

½ cup [75 g] unbleached all-purpose flour

¼ tsp fine sea salt

Scant 1 cup [240 ml] warm water

Vegetable oil for brushing and frying

Good-quality runny honey or confectioners' sugar for garnish

2 Tbsp slivered or chopped pistachios (optional)

◆ I have put *crêpes* in quotation marks because these are not made with batter as crêpes are, but rather with a malleable dough that is stretched thin, folded, and fried to produce the most scrumptious crisp pastries, which can be sweetened with honey or confectioners' sugar. They are not normally garnished with nuts, but I like to scatter pistachios over them to add another layer of flavor and texture. The "crêpes" do take a little time to prepare but they are totally worth it.

Combine the semolina, flour, and salt in a mixing bowl and gradually add the water. Knead until you have a rough ball of dough. Transfer to a lightly floured surface and knead for 3 minutes. Roll the dough into a ball. Invert the mixing bowl over the dough and let rest for 15 minutes. This resting time will facilitate the hydration of the dough and shorten the kneading time. Uncover the dough and knead for another 3 minutes.

Divide the dough into 12 balls, each the size of an egg. Brush each with vegetable oil and place on a baking sheet. Cover loosely with plastic wrap.

Put a little vegetable oil in a bowl and keep it handy for flattening the dough. Smear your work surface with oil.

Pick up a ball of dough and lay it on the oiled surface. Dip your fingers in oil and start flattening the dough, gently pulling on the edges until you have a very thin circle, about 6 in [15 cm] in diameter. Pick up the top edge and bring it to the middle of the circle. Do the same with the sides and the bottom to form a square. Lay on a baking sheet and shape the rest of the dough.

Pour enough vegetable oil into a large, deep frying pan to reach a depth of 1 in [2.5 cm]. Place over medium heat. Check the temperature by dropping a little batter into the oil; if the oil bubbles around it, it's ready. (A candy thermometer should register 350°F [180°C].) Slide one shaped dough piece into the pan.

Fry the "crêpe" until golden all over, 2 to 3 minutes on each side. Using a slotted spoon, transfer the crispy "crêpe" to a wire rack set over a large baking sheet and let the excess oil drain off. Repeat with the remaining dough pieces one at a time, making sure the oil does not get too hot.

The "crêpes" are best eaten immediately, but you can store them in an airtight container at room temperature for up to 1 day. Drizzle with the honey or sprinkle with the confectioners' sugar and scatter the pistachios (if using) over the top only when you are ready to serve them.

SMID

semolina

Ground from durum wheat, semolina comes in both fine and regular grades and is used in sweets to create a pastry that is crumblier and has more texture than that made with flour. Semolina is also boiled with milk to make a custardlike filling for some desserts.

braided sesame pastries

MAKES ABOUT **30** PASTRIES

pastry

Pinch of saffron threads

2 Tbsp orange blossom water

1¼ cups [125 g] sesame seeds

1⅔ cups [250 g] unbleached all-purpose flour

Pinch of fine sea salt

⅛ tsp ground cinnamon

1 tsp fast-acting (instant) yeast

1 large egg, beaten

1 Tbsp white wine vinegar

3 Tbsp unsalted butter, melted

⅓ cup plus 1 Tbsp [100 ml] warm water

syrup

4 small grains mastic (see page 55), crushed in a small mortar with a pestle to yield ¼ tsp powdered mastic

3 cups [750 g] good-quality runny honey

2 Tbsp orange blossom water

Sunflower oil for frying

◆ *Ch'bakiya* is the quintessential Ramadan (Muslim month of fasting) pastry in Morocco, served throughout the month with *harira*, a savory soup that is another Ramadan staple and the first thing Moroccans eat when they break their fast after sunset. The combination of the lemony soup and the sweet, crunchy pastry is unusual but quite delicious, and the pastries are well worth making even if they are a little time-consuming. Some cooks add ground almonds and ground aniseed to the pastry, but I like the texture and flavor of the pastry in this recipe. In Morocco, there are often two people involved in the preparation of *ch'bakiya*, one who continuously kneads the dough and another who shapes and fries it. I recommend that you enlist a friend, your partner, or even a keen youngster to help you. Not only will it make preparing the *ch'bakiya* easier but it will also be a lot more fun. And in the end, you will have the prettiest and most scrumptious pastries to offer with coffee and tea, or to take to friends as a gift. And of course, you can also serve them Moroccan style with *harira* soup.

To make the pastry: Crush the saffron threads between your fingers or in a small mortar using a pestle. Put the crushed saffron in a small bowl and add the orange blossom water. Set aside to infuse.

continued

Put the sesame seeds in a nonstick frying pan and place over medium heat. Toast the seeds, stirring continuously, until golden, about 10 minutes. Let cool, and then put half in a coffee or spice grinder reserved for nuts and seeds, or use the small bowl of your food processor and grind until very fine (this will take a few minutes). Reserve the other half for the garnish.

Put the flour in a mixing bowl. Add the ground sesame seeds, sea salt, cinnamon, and yeast and mix well. Add the saffron water, egg, vinegar, and melted butter. Work them into the flour mixture using the tips of your fingers. Gradually add the warm water and knead well for about 10 minutes until you have a smooth dough. If you have a stand mixer, by all means use it. I do this by hand.

Butter your work surface and rolling pin. Pinch off a piece of dough the size of a tangerine and roll it out thinly, about 2 mm thick. Cut into strips measuring about 4 in [10 cm] long by 1 in [2 cm] wide. Lift three strips and press the tops together. Braid the strips loosely and press the bottom ends together. Shape loosely into a round and press the ends together well so that the pastry does not unroll during cooking. Place on a plate and continue shaping the pastries, making sure you use up all the loose pieces.

To make the syrup: Stir the crushed mastic with the honey and orange blossom water in a deep saucepan. Place over medium heat, bring to a gentle bubble, and immediately turn the heat to very low to keep the honey hot and liquid.

Pour enough sunflower oil into a large, deep frying pan to reach a depth of 1½ in [4 cm]. Place over medium-high heat. Check the temperature by dropping a piece of dough into the oil; if the oil bubbles around it, it's ready. (A candy thermometer should register 350°F [180°C].) Drop in as many pastries as will fit comfortably without crowding.

Fry until browned all over, about 3 minutes, turning them several times.

Remove the pastries using a slotted spoon and drop them into the hot honey. Leave them for a few minutes, and then transfer to a serving dish. Repeat the process, making sure the oil does not get too hot. Sprinkle both sides of the finished pastries with the remaining toasted sesame seeds and let cool before serving.

mastic

Mastic is a dried resin that seeps out of the bark of the *Pistacia lentiscus* (the same genus as pistachios), an evergreen tree native to the Mediterranean basin. Mastic is harvested in July and August. Producers go to the fields early in the morning to make incisions in the trees, allowing the resin to seep out—a process called *kentima*. The transparent resin is then collected and rinsed in barrels, after which it is spread out and left to dry before being sorted by hand.

There are two kinds of dried mastic: clear, tiny grains called *dahtilidopetres* (flintstones), and the larger, spotted soft ones known as *kantiles* (blisters). The latter is the coarser grade. It is normally used for chewing—the resin is a natural chewing gum (*mastic* derives from the ancient Greek "to chew")—while the finer grade is used in cooking. These days, however,

it is becoming more and more difficult to purchase "flintstones." Most mastic that is available now is the "blisters" type. In the summer of 2012, the fires on the Greek island of Chios, the world's main producer of mastic. burned half the trees, so there is now a lot less mastic available.

Some mastic grains are very large, and when I call for grains in recipes, I mean those that are smaller than half the size of a cannellini bean. Reserve a small mortar and pestle that you use only for mastic so as not to corrupt the flavor, and crush the grains on demand. If you crush more than you need, simply wrap your mortar with plastic wrap and keep until you next need the mastic, or you can transfer to a jar for storage. I keep mine in the refrigerator, but that's not necessary. Mastic will keep for up to 1 year.

sesame seeds

Considered the oldest oilseed crop known to humankind, sesame was first used domestically more than five thousand years ago. In some places, it is known as a survivor crop because it is very drought tolerant and can grow where most crops fail. Sesame seeds, both raw and toasted, are widely used around the world in both

sweet and savory dishes. You can buy the seeds ready-toasted or you can dry-toast them yourself in a pan over medium heat. You need to stir them all the time to make sure they do not burn, taking the pan off the heat just before they reach the right color, continuing to stir because they will keep browning from the heat of the pan.

pistachio-filled semolina pastries

MAKES ABOUT **15** PASTRIES

pastry

1 cup [175 g] semolina (regular, not fine)

2 Tbsp unbleached all-purpose flour

2 Tbsp superfine sugar

⅛ tsp fast-acting (instant) yeast

5 Tbsp [75 g] unsalted butter, at room temperature

1½ Tbsp orange blossom water

1½ Tbsp rose water

filling

¾ cup [100 g] hulled unsalted pistachios

2 Tbsp superfine sugar

¾ tsp orange blossom water

¾ tsp rose water

Confectioners' sugar or Sweet Soapwort Dip (page 59)

◆ Throughout the Middle East, souks are divided by trade, with each trade having its own section. In Damascus's Madhat Pasha souk, located on Straight Street where Saint Paul had his epiphany, there is a section devoted to kitchen equipment, with shops selling everything from whisks to pots and pans to baking equipment—basically the Arab equivalent of Sur la Table. There are only four shops and in each there are men busy shaping metal *sajs* (inverted woks on which to bake flat breads) or carving wooden molds called *tabe'*, used to shape *ma'mul*, a confection associated with Ramadan for Muslims and Easter for Christians. The molds are beautiful, with intricate geometric patterns. Each shape announces the filling inside the pastry: oval and pointed pastries are filled with pistachios, round and pointed are filled with walnuts, and round and flat have date filling. The recipe I give here is for the pistachio-filled *ma'mul*. Don't worry if you don't have the mold to shape them. You can do this by hand and use tweezers to pinch patterns on the surface.

Sweet Soapwort Dip is great with the pastries; you eat them dipped in a little bit (or a lot, in my case) to add creaminess and sweetness. If you are going to serve them together, there is no need to sprinkle the cookies with confectioners' sugar, as suggested. You can also serve the dip with any other cookies that take your fancy, as long as they are not too sweet.

continued

To make the pastry: Mix the semolina, flour, sugar, and yeast in a mixing bowl. Add the butter and, with the tips of your fingers, work it in until fully incorporated. Add the orange blossom water and rose water and knead until the pastry is smooth and elastic. (Add a drop more rose water if you find the pastry a little dry.) Place in a lightly floured bowl. Cover with plastic wrap and let rest in a cool place for 1½ hours.

To make the filling: Using a spice grinder or small food processor, grind the pistachios to a medium-fine texture. Mix the ground pistachios and sugar in a mixing bowl. Add the orange blossom water and rose water and mix well.

Preheat the oven to 400°F [200°C]. Line a baking sheet with parchment paper or a silicone baking mat.

Pinch off a small piece of pastry and roll it into a ball the size of a walnut. Place it in your palm and flatten with your fingers, until you have an oval about 3 in [7.5 cm] long, about 2 in [5 cm] wide in the middle, and about ¼ in [6 mm] thick. Place 1 tsp of pistachio filling in a line down the middle lengthwise and pinch the dough together to close it over the filling.

Carefully shape the filled pastry into a finger with a fat middle and if you have a *tabe'*, lightly press the pastry into it, leaving the pinched side on the outside (so that when you invert the molded pastry, it is on the bottom). Place the fingers of your other hand under a work surface with your palm protruding. Invert the mold over your hand and tap the mold lightly against the work surface to release the pastry into your palm. Slide the pastry onto the prepared baking sheet. Fill and shape the remaining pastry in the same way. You may have to scrape the inside of the mold every now and then in case some pastry sticks to it. If you don't have a *tabe'*, gently shape the pastry between the palms of your hands to create a flat oval bottom, mounding the *ma'mul* into a rounded sloping shape. You should end up with about 15 pastries, each measuring about 3 in [7.5 cm] long, 1 in [2.5 cm] wide in the middle, and 1¼ in [3 cm] high.

Bake the pastries until cooked and barely colored, 12 to 15 minutes. Transfer to a wire rack. Let cool, and then sprinkle with confectioners' sugar before serving.

sweet soapwort dip

MAKES **2** CUPS [**480** ML]

2 oz [55 g] soapwort root, rinsed well under cold water

2½ cups [600 ml] water

1½ cups [360 ml] Fragrant Sugar Syrup (page 46)

◆ The dried roots of *Saponaria officinalis* and *Gypsophila struthium* are known as *shirsh al-halawa* in Arabic. The roots are boiled in water, strained out, and the water is whisked into a stiff white foam—an extraordinary transformation, thanks to the roots' *saponin* (soap) content. The foam is then whisked with sugar syrup to make *natef*, a soft meringue-like dip. Soon after the publication of my book on Lebanese cuisine, Helen Saberi, Esteban Pombo-Villar, Alan Davidson, and I investigated whether *shirsh al-halawa* is soapwort or if it is *bois de Panama* (an extract from the *Quillaja saponaria*, or soapbark tree). Our results were published in the journal *Petits Propos Culinaires*, and later reprinted in *The Wilder Shores of Gastronomy*. We concluded *shirsh al-halawa* is indeed soapwort, although you can also use *bois de Panama* as a substitute to make *natef*.

Whenever I make *natef*, I anxiously wonder if the brown water will ever really whisk into a fluffy white cloud. It unfailingly does. Many sweets makers now make *natef* with egg white, but I consider this cheating and never buy *natef* unless it is made with soapwort root.

In a saucepan over medium heat, bring the soapwort and water to a boil; watch, as it will foam up and could boil over. Simmer until the liquid is reduced to ½ cup plus 2 Tbsp [150 ml]; by then it will have become brown.

Strain the soapwort liquid into a large mixing bowl or the bowl of a stand mixer and, using an electric beater or a whisk attachment, beat until the water has turned into a white, shiny foam.

Gradually whisk the sugar syrup into the foam by hand until you have a fluffy, stretchy meringue-like mixture. The more powerful your whisking, the better the *natef* will be and the longer it will last without separating. Store, covered, in the refrigerator for up to 1 week. If you find that the mixture has separated, whisk it to recombine.

date-filled pastries

MAKES **45** TO **50** PASTRIES

honey syrup

1⅔ cups [400 ml] water

1¾ cups [350 g] organic cane sugar

⅓ cup [100 g] honey

pastry

Pinch of saffron threads

1 cup [240 ml] warm water

2½ cups [450 g] fine semolina

¼ tsp fine sea salt

¼ tsp baking soda

¼ cup [60 ml] extra-virgin olive oil

filling

1½ cups [225 g] pitted dates

2 Tbsp extra-virgin olive oil

¼ tsp ground cinnamon

Grated zest of 1 orange

Sunflower oil for frying

◆ Originally from Al-Qayrawan (also known as Kairouan), Tunisia, these flattened pastries are luscious. The meltingly soft date filling coupled with the final dip in honey syrup contrasts nicely with the crumbly semolina pastry. Deep-frying them until crisp and golden doubles the scrumptiousness. Once the pastries are filled, they are pressed with a special stamp to both flatten them and create a ridged design on the dough. You are unlikely to find the stamp outside Al-Qayrawan, but you can simply flatten the filled dough with your fingers and use the side of a box grater to leave a fish-scale pattern in the dough. The pastries may not end up as well shaped or as attractive as those made with the special stamp, but the taste will be just as delectable. You can also try using a cookie stamp.

To make the syrup: In a medium saucepan, combine the water, sugar, and honey and bring to a boil over medium heat, stirring occasionally. Simmer for 3 minutes, remove from the heat, and let cool to room temperature.

To make the pastry: Crush the saffron threads between your fingers or in a small mortar with a pestle. In a small bowl, combine the saffron with the water and set aside to infuse for 15 minutes.

In a large mixing bowl, combine the semolina, salt, and baking soda; mix well, then make a well in the center. Add the olive oil and the saffron water and stir with your hand or a spatula to incorporate the wet and dry ingredients. Knead in the bowl by hand until you have a smooth, malleable dough. Cover with plastic wrap and let rest for 15 minutes.

To make the filling: While the dough is resting, in a food processor, pulse the dates until coarsely chopped. Add the olive oil, cinnamon, and orange zest and process until the mixture forms a smooth paste, about 1 minute, scraping down the bowl as needed. Divide the filling into 12 equal pieces. Shape each piece into a cylinder about ¾ in [2 cm] thick and 2 in [5 cm] long and set on a plate or baking sheet. Cover with plastic wrap.

Lightly oil a baking sheet (or use a nonstick baking sheet). Place a wire rack over a second baking sheet.

Divide the dough into 12 equal pieces and shape each piece into a ball. Roll one ball of dough into an oval about 4 in [10 cm] in length, 2 in [5 cm] wide, and ½ in [12 mm] thick. Place a filling cylinder along the length of the dough oval, centered over one half. Fold the other half over, enclosing the filling. Using your fingers or the fine-holed side of a box grater, flatten the filled dough to an even ½-in [12-mm] thickness. Using a chef's knife, trim the ends, and then cut the dough at an angle into diamonds with about 1-in [2.5-cm] sides; you should be able to cut four diamonds. Lay them on the oiled baking sheet. Repeat with the remaining dough and filling.

Pour enough sunflower oil into a larger, deep frying pan to reach a depth of 2 in [5 cm]. Place over medium heat. Check the temperature by dropping in a piece of dough into the oil; if the oil bubbles around it, it's ready. (A candy thermometer should register 350°F [180°C].) Drop in as many pastries as will comfortably fit without overcrowding.

Fry the pastries until golden all over, 2 to 3 minutes on each side.

Remove the pastries using a slotted spoon and drop them into the syrup. Turn a few times in the syrup to coat them well, and then transfer to the prepared rack to allow the excess syrup to drain off.

Fry and coat the remaining pastries in the same way, making sure the oil does not get too hot. Let cool on the rack to room temperature. Store in an airtight container at room temperature for up to 3 days.

semolina cream hand pies

SERVES **4**

5 Tbsp [50 g] semolina (regular, not fine)

2 cups [480 ml] whole milk

¼ cup [50 g] superfine sugar

1 Tbsp orange blossom water

9 oz [250 g] store-bought all-butter puff pastry

Unbleached all-purpose flour for rolling out the pastry

1 large egg yolk beaten with 1 tsp water

Confectioners' sugar for dusting

◆ *Tamriye* means "made with dates" in Arabic, an odd name for a dish that contains no dates. There must be an explanation, though I have been unable to find it. What I do know is that it is a dessert with strong religious associations. Greek Orthodox Christians prepare it for the day of Saint Matthew (Mar Metr), while Maronites have it to celebrate the Assumption of the Virgin (Eid al-Saydeh). It is traditionally prepared with a dough so thin that you should be able to read a newspaper through it; the dough is fried and sprinkled with confectioners' sugar. I am neither patient nor particularly good at rolling out dough so thin. In fact, the sweets makers don't even roll out the dough. Instead they flap it in the air in a rotating motion to stretch and thin it out. I have devised another way, using good-quality commercial puff pastry, which saves time and creates a crisper shell than the traditional pastry.

Put the semolina, milk, and superfine sugar in a saucepan and place over medium heat. Bring to a boil, whisking constantly. Turn the heat to low and continue whisking for 5 minutes longer. Add the orange blossom water and whisk for another minute or so. Remove from the heat and pour into a 6½-in [16-cm] square dish, spreading the mixture evenly about ½ in [12 mm] thick. Let cool completely before cutting into 1½-in [4-cm] squares. You should have 16 pieces.

Preheat the oven to 400°F [200°C]. Line a baking sheet with parchment paper or a silicone baking mat.

Roll out the puff pastry thinly, sprinkling it with all-purpose flour so that it doesn't stick. Cut it into 16 pieces, each 4 in [10 cm] square. Place a semolina piece in the middle of each square, pick up one corner, and flap it over the filling, positioning the corner in the middle of the square. Pick up the opposite corner and flap it over the first; do the same with the other two corners. Press the folded pastry lightly into the filling and place on the prepared baking sheet. Continue filling and shaping the pastry until you have 16 filled packets. Brush them with the beaten egg yolk mixture.

Bake until light golden, 15 to 20 minutes. Transfer to a wire rack and let cool. The pies are best served the day they are made, but keep reasonably well in an airtight container at room temperature for up to 2 days. Serve warm or at room temperature, dusted with confectioners' sugar.

walnut phyllo triangles

MAKES **12** TRIANGLES

filling

¾ cup [75 g] walnuts

Scant 1 Tbsp superfine sugar

Scant ¼ tsp ground cinnamon

½ tsp orange blossom water

½ tsp rose water

8 sheets phyllo pastry, each measuring 11 by 17 in [28 by 43 cm]

5 Tbsp [75 g] unsalted butter, melted

¾ cup [180 ml] Fragrant Sugar Syrup (page 46)

◆ This is a take on baklava: the phyllo is used to make individual triangles that can be filled with nut filling, as in this recipe, or else with *qashta* (clotted cream; see page 31), unsalted cheese, or milk pudding (see Variation). Whichever version you choose to make, you will end up with totally scrumptious triangles. If you want just a few at a time, you can make the whole recipe and freeze the triangles before baking; take out however many you wish and let them thaw before baking.

Preheat the oven to 400°F [200°C]. Line a large baking sheet with parchment paper or a silicone baking mat.

To make the filling: Put the walnuts in a food processor and process until medium-fine. Transfer to a mixing bowl. Add the sugar, cinnamon, orange blossom water, and rose water; mix well.

Lay one sheet of phyllo pastry on your work surface (keep the other sheets covered with plastic wrap and a clean kitchen towel to keep them from drying out) and brush with a little melted butter. Lay on another sheet of phyllo, brush with butter, and continue with another two layers, brushing each with butter. Cut the layered sheets into 3½-in [9-cm] squares. Separate one stacked square and spread a heaping 1 tsp of walnut filling in the middle, leaving the edges clear. Fold the pastry over the filling to make a triangle and press the edges together. Brush the top and bottom with butter and place on the prepared baking sheet. Continue making the rest of the triangles, arranging them on the baking sheet.

Bake until crisp and golden brown, 10 to 15 minutes. Let cool on the baking sheet for a couple of minutes, and then drizzle the sugar syrup over the triangles. Serve immediately, or let cool to serve at room temperature (they are best eaten soon after they are prepared).

Variation: Make milk pudding by mixing ½ cup plus 2 Tbsp [150 ml] milk, 6 Tbsp [90 ml] heavy cream, and 2 Tbsp cornstarch in a small saucepan. Bring to a boil over medium heat, whisking constantly, and boil for 3 to 5 minutes, still whisking. Let cool to room temperature before using in place of the walnut filling.

almond-orange triangles

MAKES ABOUT **24** TRIANGLES

plain sugar syrup

2 cups [400 g] superfine sugar

1 tsp freshly squeezed lemon juice

½ cup [120 ml] water

filling

1⅔ cups [250 g] blanched almonds, lightly toasted (see page 25)

¼ cup [35 g] confectioners' sugar

½ tsp grated orange zest

1 egg white, lightly beaten

2 Tbsp rose water

¼ cup [25 g] sesame seeds

12 sheets *brik* (see facing page) or phyllo pastry

7 Tbsp [100 g] unsalted butter, melted (if using phyllo)

Sunflower oil for frying

◆ These are both crunchy and moist at the same time. The thinnest pastry is wrapped around finely ground nuts to form triangles that are fried and then dipped in sugar syrup. The pastry stays crisp while the nuts sop up the syrup, resulting in a wonderful contrast of crunchy and soft in each bite, which makes *samsa* totally irresistible. In Morocco, Tunisia, and Algeria, the pastry normally used is *warqa* or *malsuqa*, also known as *brik*, but you can use phyllo. The size of phyllo sheets varies according to the brand. The Greek and Turkish brands are generally larger and thinner than supermarket brands.

To make the sugar syrup: Put the superfine sugar, lemon juice, and water in a saucepan and place over medium heat. Bring to a boil, stirring occasionally. Boil for 3 minutes, and then remove from the heat. Let cool before using. The syrup will keep for up to 2 weeks in the refrigerator; bring to room temperature before using.

To make the filling: Grind the toasted almonds in a food processor until very fine. Transfer to a mixing bowl. Add the confectioners' sugar, orange zest, egg white, and rose water; blend well. Set aside.

Put the sesame seeds in a nonstick frying pan and place over medium heat. Toast the seeds, stirring continuously, until golden, about 10 minutes. Let cool.

Cut one sheet of pastry in half. If using *brik*, fold the round side over to form a long rectangle. If using phyllo sheets, cut into long strips that are 5 in [12.5 cm] wide; fold the strips in half lengthwise and brush with melted butter.

Place 2 to 3 tsp of almond filling at the top of each strip of pastry. Fold the top corner over the filling to form a triangle and continue folding as though folding a flag until the filling is completely encased in the triangle. Tuck the end corner in, place on a plate, and continue filling and shaping the triangles until you use up both filling and pastry.

Pour enough sunflower oil into a large, deep frying pan to reach a depth of 2 in [5 cm]. Place over medium-high heat. Check the temperature by dipping the corner of one pastry into the oil; if the oil bubbles around it, it's ready. (A candy thermometer should register 350°F [180°C].) Drop in about four pastries; don't crowd the pan, or later the syrup.

Fry the pastries until golden brown all over, a couple of minutes on each side. Remove the pastries using a slotted spoon and drop them into the syrup. Turn in the syrup a couple of times and transfer to a serving dish. Repeat the process, making sure the oil doesn't get too hot. Once you have done all the *samsa*, sprinkle them with the toasted sesame seeds. Store in an airtight container at room temperature for up to 3 days.

warqa or brik

Warqa (meaning "leaf" in Arabic) is the North African equivalent of phyllo and is used to make various sweet and savory pastries. The Tunisians call it *malsuqa* (meaning "glued"). Making *warqa* or *malsuqa* requires special skill, or at least a lot of practice. I once tried making *warqa* under the guidance of the late Boujemaa Mars, the venerable former head chef at the Mammounia Hotel in Marrakesh. Even though my first and only attempt was not an abject failure, it showed me that it would take very many more trials for me to master the art of making *warqa*. What I do now is buy either commercially produced *brik* when I find it or excellent handmade ones in the souks or at bakeries on my travels to Morocco or Tunisia, which I freeze as soon as I get home. You can find *brik* in Middle Eastern stores; if not available, phyllo pastry or thin *yufka* (see page 73) make a good substitute.

almond spirals

MAKES **20** LARGE OR **40** DAINTY PASTRIES

filling

3¾ cups [500 g] blanched almonds

1¼ cups [150 g] confectioners' sugar

¼ cup [60 ml] orange blossom water

2 Tbsp unsalted butter, at room temperature

6 to 8 grains mastic (see page 55), finely ground in a small mortar with a pestle to yield ½ tsp powdered mastic

One 14-oz [400-g] package phyllo pastry (the sheets I used measured 11½ by 16¾ in [29 by 42 cm])

½ cup plus 2 Tbsp [150 g] unsalted butter, melted

◆ A variation on the Gazelle's Horns (page 102), these spirals have the almond paste wrapped in *warqa* (the Moroccan equivalent of phyllo; see page 69) and shaped into a coil before being baked until slightly crisp and lightly colored. They are much quicker to prepare than Gazelle's Horns, and if you cannot find *warqa* (or *brik*, as the pastry is also known), simply use a very thin Greek or Turkish phyllo. You can, if you want, make the almond rolls much thinner to yield forty pastries instead of twenty. They look prettier, but I often make them larger because they take less time.

To make the filling: Place the almonds in a heatproof bowl; pour in enough boiling water to cover and let sit for 1 hour. Drain the almonds well and dry them with a clean kitchen towel.

Combine the almonds with the confectioners' sugar in a food processor. Process until very finely ground, about 2 minutes. Add the orange blossom water, butter, and mastic and process until well blended. Transfer the paste to your work surface and roll into a sausage shape. Divide into 20 equal pieces and shape each piece into first a ball and then into a thin cylinder measuring about 9 in [22.5 cm] long. Cover with plastic wrap.

Preheat the oven to 400°F [200°C]. Line a baking sheet with parchment paper or a silicone baking mat.

continued

Lay one sheet of phyllo on your work surface and brush with a little melted butter. Lay one almond cylinder about ½ in [12 mm] away from the edge nearest you, and about ¾ in [2 cm] away from the edges of the phyllo. Flap the phyllo over the almond cylinder and roll, keeping the phyllo very close to the filling as you roll the pastry over it. Brush with butter and, with the seam side down, fold one empty end over the almond roll and roll into a spiral, sliding the other empty end under the coil.

Transfer the coil to the prepared baking sheet and press lightly on it to make sure it doesn't unroll during baking. Make the remaining spirals the same way. When you have finished them, poke each one here and there with a toothpick to keep the pastry from puffing.

Bake until golden, 25 minutes. Let cool on a wire rack. Store in an airtight container at room temperature for up to 1 week.

phyllo pastry

Phyllo is the name Greeks use to describe dough of any kind, not only the very thin sheets of dough we know as phyllo. Despite the Greek name, the origin of phyllo is Turkish. An eleventh-century dictionary of local Turkish dialects (*Diwan Lughat al-Turk*) recorded "pleated or folded bread" as one meaning for the word *yurgha*, archaic for *yufka*, which is the Turkish name for phyllo. *Yufka* also refers to sheets of thin dough of various thicknesses, none of which can be described as thick. In Arab countries, phyllo is known as *reqaqat* ("thinned out" in Arabic).

Before World War I, elegant households in Istanbul kept two phyllo makers, one to make the thin sheets for baklava and the other to make the thicker sheets used in *böreks*. Though less common nowadays, there are many traditional households in Turkey that still make phyllo at home.

More and more contemporary professional bakers use mechanical rollers because the rollers are less labor-intensive. Whether by hand or by machine, the work is done in a room dedicated to both rolling out the pastry and shaping the different types of baklava. The men in charge—and these professional kitchens are truly a man's world—work at long rectangular tables with marble tops cloaked in clouds of cornstarch, used to keep the sheets of pastry from sticking to each other. The bakers start by rolling out balls of dough into thick disks measuring about 10 in [25 cm] across, which are then stacked and sprinkled with cornstarch. Each stack will have more than 12 disks. To stretch the sheets by hand, the men use very long, straight wooden rolling pins to roll out the stack until the sheets are ten times the width they were and so thin you can read a newspaper through them. Then they roll their sheets around the rolling pin and stretch the sheets further by cupping their hands around them and gently pulling the roll of pastry up and down.

When the rolling out is done by machine, the man in charge of the rolling machine places one stack in the center of a large wooden table and lowers a plastic mechanical roller that is almost as wide as the table onto the stack. The roller goes back and forth over the stack, each time pressing it down to stretch the dough. The wooden table swivels a quarter turn with each rolling out so that the sheets are flattened to a perfect circle. Once the pastry sheets have been stretched almost as wide as the table, the baker rolls the sheets onto a large rolling pin and hands it to a young boy to take to those in charge of shaping the baklava or other sweets.

You can find excellent commercial phyllo and *yufka* at Middle Eastern markets or by mail order. Phyllo sheets tear easily, and they dry very quickly if not kept covered—I cover with plastic wrap and a kitchen towel over that.

baklava

SERVES 4

filling

1⅓ cups [200 g] hulled unsalted pistachios

½ cup [100 g] superfine sugar

1 Tbsp orange blossom water

1 Tbsp rose water

12 sheets phyllo pastry, each measuring 7 by 12½ in [18 by 32 cm]

5 Tbsp [75 g] unsalted butter, melted

6 Tbsp [90 ml] Fragrant Sugar Syrup (page 46)

◆ The term *baklava* is generic, referring to a whole selection of sweets made with either phyllo or "hair" pastry (see page 81). Most of those made with phyllo are known as *kol wa shkor* (eat and be thankful), whereas those made with "hair" pastry are known under different names: *borma* (meaning "twist" and describing long rolls of hair pastry wrapping pistachios) or *balluriyeh* (a white, square version of *borma*). The best baklava is made by specialists, as it is not so easy to make at home. However, it is very satisfying to make your own even if it will not be as exquisite as that made by the professionals. Here, I give a recipe for a simple version made with phyllo. Although the pros roll out their own phyllo, store-bought phyllo works fine.

Preheat the oven to 400°F [200°C]. Butter a medium baking dish measuring about 7 by 12½ by 1¼ in [18 by 32 by 3 cm].

To make the filling: Coarsely grind the pistachios in a spice grinder or small food processor and transfer to a mixing bowl. Add the sugar, orange blossom water, and rose water; mix well. Set aside.

Spread one sheet of phyllo pastry over the bottom of the prepared baking dish. (Keep the other sheets covered with plastic wrap and a clean kitchen towel over that so the phyllo doesn't dry out.) Brush with melted butter. Lay another sheet over the first and brush with more melted butter; repeat with an addtional four sheets, brushing each with butter for a total of six layers of phyllo. Spread the pistachio filling evenly over the pastry and cover with six more layers of phyllo, brushing each one with melted butter. Pour any leftover butter over the pastry.

Cut the pastry into 2-in [5-cm] squares or into thin rectangles about 2 in [5 cm] long and ¾ in [2 cm] wide.

Bake until crisp and golden, 15 to 20 minutes. Remove from the oven and let sit for a minute or two before pouring the sugar syrup all over the pastry. Store in an airtight container at room temperature for up to 2 days.

Variation: You can vary the shape by making rolls that are cut into short fingers before baking. Lay one sheet of phyllo on your work surface with the long side facing you. Brush with melted butter and arrange one-twelfth of the nut filling in a thin line all along the long side nearest to you, about ½ in [12 mm] away from the edge. Flip the edge over the filling and carefully roll the pastry to make a long, thin sausage. Brush the roll with melted butter and carefully lift it, placing it on the baking dish against the long edge. Make the remaining rolls in the same way, aligning them against the first roll until you have filled the baking dish. Cut the rolls into 2-in [5-cm] fingers and proceed as directed.

sweet cheese pie

SERVES **4** TO **6**

11 oz [300 g] **Akkawi cheese or cow's-milk mozzarella**

9 oz [250 g] *qataifi* **("hair" pastry; see page 81)**

7 Tbsp [100 g] **unsalted butter, diced**

1½ cups [360 ml] **Fragrant Sugar Syrup (page 46)**

◆ This rich and luxurious cheese pie is made by layering desalted cheese with *qataifi* ("hair" pastry), as it is known in Arabic. In some parts of the Middle East and Turkey, the pastry is left whole, whereas in Lebanon it is crumbled to resemble coarse semolina. It is one of the great Middle Eastern confections, satisfying and incredibly delicious, and it's one of the first things I rush to eat when I go back home to Lebanon. This recipe is for the Lebanese version, but if you want to make the other version, see the Variation. Look for Akkawi cheese, a semihard white brine cheese, at Middle Eastern markets. This pie is often served with sesame galettes.

Slice the cheese about ½ in [12 mm] thick and soak in cold water, changing the water every 15 minutes or so, until the cheese has lost all trace of saltiness, about 2 hours. Drain.

Preheat the oven to 400°F [200°C]. Butter a 9-in [23-cm] round baking dish.

Chop the *qataifi* into ½-in [12-mm] pieces and put in a wide pan. Make a well in the middle and add the diced butter. Place the pan over low heat and rub the melting butter into the pastry with your hands until all the pastry shreds are well coated and the butter has melted completely. This will take a few minutes.

Spread the shredded pastry across the prepared dish in an even layer. Press it down with your hands.

Bake until crisp and light golden, 5 to 10 minutes.

continued

Remove the pastry from the oven and spread the drained cheese slices evenly over it. Bake for 10 to 15 minutes more, or until the cheese has melted completely and the pastry underneath is golden brown. Alternatively, you can cook the pie on top of the stove, which is what Lebanese bakers do. Spread the cheese slices over the pastry and place the baking dish over low heat. Cook for about 20 minutes, turning the dish regularly to make sure the bottom of the pastry browns evenly. When done, the pie should move in one block as you shake the dish from side to side.

Serve hot or warm. Drizzle a little sugar syrup all over the pastry and serve with more syrup on the side. The pie is not good cold; the cheese needs to be melting. Ideally, you should turn the pie over onto a serving dish that has been brushed with a little sugar syrup to keep the cheese from sticking. You can also cut the pie into 3-in [7.5-cm] squares and serve these upside down on a platter (also brushed with syrup) to show off the golden pastry. However, because the pastry is quite crumbly, the presentation will not be as pretty as if you turn over the whole pie.

Variation: For the whole-pastry version, don't rub the *qataifi* to break it up once you have added the butter. Instead, simply toss the shreds to coat them with the butter, and then lay half the *qataifi* on the bottom of the dish. Spread the cheese over it and cover with the remaining *qataifi*; bake until golden brown. I favor the Lebanese version, but this style is a little quicker to prepare.

"hair" pastry

"Hair" pastry, known as *qataifi* or *sha'r* in Arabic, is also used for baklava. As with phyllo pastry, the process of making it can be either partly automated or completely by hand.

One time, in Gaziantep, Turkey, I spotted a *qataifi* maker opposite the hotel where I was staying. I had already seen the pastry being made in Syria, where the batter is poured into a long, horizontal funnel with tiny holes along the bottom through which the batter falls onto a hot plate. I was curious if the Turks made it the same way and was very surprised to see it made entirely by hand with the help of a small, rather beautiful metal container fitted with a row of mini funnels on the bottom. The pastry maker held the cup using one finger to block the holes, and once he'd poured the batter into the cup, he released his finger and, with amazing speed and precision, rotated the cup around and around over the hot metal plate, dropping the finest strands of batter, which sizzled as soon as they hit the plate. Once he covered the plate, with a deft movement he picked up the strands of pastry, laid them on a cloth, and started again.

"Hair" pastry is used to make several dishes, including the Sweet Cheese Pie called *kunafa* (page 78) that is normally eaten for breakfast, and *borma*, in which the pastry is rolled around pistachios to form cylinders that are then fried and dipped in syrup before being cut into pieces. "Hair" pastry is available frozen at Middle Eastern stores.

cakes and cookies

turkish pistachio cake

SERVES **8** TO **10**

Heaping 1 cup [150 g] hulled unsalted pistachios

5 large eggs, at room temperature, separated

1 cup [200 g] organic cane sugar

¾ cup [180 ml] whole-milk yogurt

½ cup [120 ml] extra-virgin olive oil

1 cup [150 g] unbleached all-purpose flour

¾ tsp baking soda

¼ tsp fine sea salt

¾ tsp cream of tartar

◆ Here is a Turkish version of sponge cake, made with yogurt and olive oil. The ground pistachios incorporated into the batter give the cake a lovely pale green color. The cake is lovely served with yogurt or crème fraîche and mixed fresh berries.

Preheat the oven to 350°F [180°C]. Butter and flour a 10-in [25-cm] round cake pan.

Spread the pistachios on a baking sheet and toast them in the oven until crisp but not browned, about 10 minutes. Remove from the oven but leave the oven on. When cool enough to handle, remove as much of the skins as you can by placing the nuts in a clean kitchen towel and rubbing between your hands. Grind the nuts in a food processor to the texture of fine bread crumbs.

Beat the egg yolks in a large mixing bowl. Add ½ cup [100 g] of the sugar and beat until the eggs have lightened and the mixture has thickened. Mix in the yogurt, followed by the olive oil.

Mix the flour with the baking soda and salt; add to the egg mixture together with the ground pistachios and mix well.

Put the egg whites in a large bowl. Add the cream of tartar and whisk until you have soft peaks. Add the remaining ½ cup [100 g] sugar and continue whisking until you have stiff peaks. Gently fold the egg whites into the batter and pour into the prepared cake pan.

Bake until the cake is golden and risen, 55 to 60 minutes. Insert a skewer and if it comes out with no crumbs attached, the cake is ready. Let cool for a few minutes, then unmold onto a wire rack to cool completely. The cake is best the day it is made.

arabian sponge cake

SERVES **6**

1 cup [150 g] unbleached all-purpose flour

1 Tbsp ground cardamom

¼ tsp saffron threads

¼ cup [60 ml] rose water

6 green cardamom pods

6 large eggs, beaten

⅔ cup [90 g] confectioners' sugar

1½ tsp baking powder

¼ tsp fine sea salt

1 Tbsp sesame seeds

◆ This exotic Arabian sponge cake is very much part of the hospitality ritual in Qatar. Whenever people visit, they are immediately offered coffee or tea together with a selection of nibbles, both sweet and savory, and *guerss al-'egaily* is often part of this hospitality menu, called *fuwala* in Arabic. The food served is a little like the cakes and sandwiches served at an English afternoon tea.

Toast the flour in a skillet over medium heat until light golden, 8 to 10 minutes. Add the ground cardamom and mix well. Let cool.

In a small bowl, combine the saffron with the rose water and let sit 15 minutes to infuse.

Open the cardamom pods and extract the seeds inside. Coarsely crush the seeds in a small mortar using a pestle.

Preheat the oven to 350°F [180°C]. Butter and flour a 6-in [15-cm] round cake pan.

Whisk the eggs with the confectioners' sugar and keep whisking until the mixture has increased in volume. Mix in the saffron–rose water mixture, and then fold in the flour mixture, baking powder, and salt and mix until completely blended. Pour the batter into the prepared pan and sprinkle the sesame seeds and coarsely crushed cardamom all over the top.

Bake until completely dry in the middle, 25 to 30 minutes. Insert a skewer and if it comes out with no crumbs attached, the cake is ready. Let cool completely before serving. Store in an airtight container at room temperature for up to 2 days.

CAKES AND COOKIES

•87•

syrian semolina and nut cake

SERVES **8** TO **10**

1¼ cups [225 g] semolina flour (regular, not fine)

6 Tbsp [85 g] unsalted butter, at room temperature

¼ cup [50 g] superfine sugar

1½ cups [360 ml] whole-milk yogurt

¼ tsp baking soda

1 tsp tahini

⅓ cup [50 g] blanched almonds

⅓ cup [50 g] hulled unsalted pistachios

⅓ cup [50 g] walnut halves

⅓ cup [50 g] unsalted cashews

1½ cups [360 ml] Fragrant Sugar Syrup (page 46), at room temperature

◆ Nabak is a little Syrian town not far from Damascus on the way to Aleppo that is famous for its *h'risseh*. I used to stop there just for this cake. The name is confusing as it also describes a Lebanese savory dish, a kind of porridge made with wheat and meat. In Syria, however, there is no mistaking the name for anything but this delectable syrupy sponge cake topped with mixed nuts. This irresistible dessert is very simple to prepare. I make mine a little less sweet than is conventional, but it still drips with sugar syrup; I love the way the sticky sweetness is tempered by the crunchy nuts.

Put the semolina, butter, and superfine sugar in a mixing bowl and work together using a spatula until well blended. Add the yogurt and baking soda and mix until you have a firm batter.

Using the tahini, grease a 10-in [25-cm] round cake pan with sides about 1¾ in [4.5 cm] high. Spread the batter evenly across the prepared pan. Flatten it gently with the back of a spoon. Cover with plastic wrap, taking care not to let the plastic touch the top of the batter, and let rest in a cool place for 3 hours.

Preheat the oven to 400°F [200°C] for about 20 minutes.

continued

Scatter the nuts all over the surface of the batter and bake until the cake is golden, 40 minutes. Remove from the oven and pour the syrup all over. Don't worry if the cake looks as if it is swimming in the syrup; it will absorb it all. Let the cake stand for 30 minutes to soak up the syrup. It may seem like too much syrup, but the cake needs it all. Of course, if you lack the Middle Eastern sweet tooth, you can decrease the amount. Store in an airtight container at room temperature for up to 1 day.

turkish pistachio shortbread

MAKES **50** PIECES

⅓ cup [50 g] hulled unsalted pistachios

½ cup plus 2 Tbsp [150 g] unsalted butter, at room temperature

1⅓ cups [150 g] confectioners' sugar

¾ cup [180 ml] sunflower oil

1 large egg, at room temperature

5 Tbsp [50 g] cornstarch

3½ cups plus 2 Tbsp [575 g] unbleached all-purpose flour

◆ Here is a delicious variation on the Lebanese and Moroccan *gh'reyba*. This dough has very finely ground pistachios added to it, which gives the shortbread a lovely pale green color, a little more texture, and a delightful nutty flavor. They may just be my favorites, especially those made by Güllüoğlu in Gaziantep.

Set aside 50 pistachios to use as garnish. Using a small food processor or spice grinder, finely grind the remaining pistachios.

Preheat the oven to 350°F [180°C]. Line two baking sheets with parchment paper or silicone baking mats.

Using an electric mixer, blend the butter and confectioners' sugar until very smooth. Add the sunflower oil and egg and mix well. Add the cornstarch and ground pistachios and combine. Finally, add the flour and mix until you have a smooth dough.

Pinch off enough dough to roll into a ball the size of a walnut. Place on the prepared baking sheet, flattening the dough slightly. Spike a pistachio in the middle. Repeat with the remaining dough.

Bake until done but not colored, 15 minutes. Let cool for a few minutes and then transfer to a wire rack to cool completely. Store in an airtight container, in a cool place, for up to 1 week.

CAKES AND COOKIES

nuts

In the Middle East, the two most important nuts are pine nuts and pistachios. The former are the edible seeds of about twenty different species of pine trees. The two most common types are from the Asian Korean pine (*Pinus koraiensis*) and the stone pine (*Pinus pinea*). Pine nuts from the Korean pine are short and fat; nuts from the stone pine are long and slim and grown around the Mediterranean, in Lebanon, Spain, and Italy. I use only the latter type because they are nicer looking and taste nuttier. Unfortunately, they are also a lot more expensive. Unshelled, pine nuts have a long shelf life, but this shortens considerably once they have been shelled. For this reason, I keep mine, alongside other nuts, in the freezer and take them out about half an hour before I need to use them.

Pistachios are one of only two types of nuts mentioned in the Bible (the other is almonds), and Pliny the Elder writes about them in his *Natural History*, mentioning how they were once unique to Syria but introduced into Italy by the Roman consul to Syria in A.D. 35. The pistachio tree (*Pistacia vera*, in the family of nut trees to which cashews and sumac also belong) is originally from Greater Iran (both Iran and Iraq), but is now grown in parts of Asia, North Africa, and the United States (in particular California), as well as in southern Europe.

The best confectioners use pistachios that the Turks call *kuş boku*, meaning "bird droppings." They are tiny and vivid green, which makes for a gorgeous filling or garnish. *Fistuq halabi*, meaning "nut of Aleppo," is the Arabic name, indicating where pistachios are grown in the region, all around Aleppo in Syria. There are also many groves around Gaziantep in southeastern Turkey. The pistachio nut grows on beautiful trees normally planted in red clay soil, which makes for a delightful landscape of gorgeous green leaves and clusters of pink nuts (the skin enveloping the shell is pink). Slivered pistachios are a lovely garnish for many sweets; they are sold in Iranian grocery stores. If you cannot find them, chopped pistachios are a fine substitution.

Another essential nut is the almond, the nut of choice in North Africa, ground and used as a filling in all kinds of confections, as well as instead of or with flour to make cookies. You can buy ground almonds (often labeled almond meal), but if I have the time, I grind my own. I may not get as fine a result as if I buy them preground, but I feel that the nuts are fresher if I process them myself.

moroccan shortbread

MAKES **30** TO **35** PIECES

1¼ cups [250 g] organic cane sugar

4 or 5 small grains mastic (see page 55), crushed in a small mortar with a pestle to yield a heaping ¼ tsp powdered mastic

2 egg yolks

1 cup plus 1 Tbsp [235 g] unsalted butter, at room temperature

3⅓ cups [500 g] unbleached all-purpose flour

⅓ cup [50 g] blanched whole almonds (optional)

◆ This shortbread, with slight variations, is found throughout the Middle East. The Moroccan version is the most aromatic because of the added mastic. Even now, many years later, I can see in my mind's eye a Berber woman sitting right on the pavement beside a caftan shop with a tray of gh'reyba in front of her, placidly waiting for passers-by to buy. They were not very prettily shaped, nor were they beautifully displayed. She just had them spread on a battered and not particularly clean metal tray. Still, there was something about her that was appealing. So I bought one and walked on. My instinct was right; her gh'reyba was excellent. I walked back, and found her still sitting quite immobile. She smiled as I bought another, and her smile grew bigger and bigger as I went back and forth several times in the next fifteen minutes, each time thinking it would be my last. We finally spoke and I asked her for the recipe, which she gave me. My adaptation does not produce quite the same crumbly texture I remember, but it's not far off. And the flavor is just as irresistible as hers.

Preheat the oven to 350°F [180°C]. Line a baking sheet with parchment paper or a silicone baking mat.

Mix the sugar and mastic in a mixing bowl and make a well in the center. Add the egg yolks and incorporate them into the sugar using a spatula. Add the butter and blend well. Gradually add the flour and knead the dough until smooth and firm. This should take about 5 minutes. (Add a little more flour if you think the dough is too soft.) Let rest in the refrigerator for 15 minutes.

Divide the dough in half and roll each piece into a fat sausage about 8 in [20 cm] long. Cut each into 15 or 17 equal pieces and roll each into a ball the size of a walnut. Flatten in your hands, leaving the top rounded, to shape a cookie measuring about 2 in [5 cm] in diameter. Press an almond into the middle and place on the prepared baking sheet. Repeat with the remaining dough.

Bake until barely colored, 15 to 20 minutes. Let cool for a few minutes and then transfer to a wire rack to cool completely. Store in an airtight container at room temperature for up to 3 days.

rice flour cookies

MAKES **28** TO **30** COOKIES

- **1 cup [220 g] unsalted butter, at room temperature**
- **2 cups [250 g] confectioners' sugar**
- **2 large eggs, at room temperature**
- **2 Tbsp rose water**
- **2⅓ cups [350 g] fine rice flour**
- **1 tsp ground cardamom**
- **1 to 2 Tbsp poppy seeds**

◆ This is an interesting Iranian variation on shortbread, made with rice flour. Iranians also use chickpea flour to make equally delectable shortbread squares, which are yellow and very crumbly, while these are creamy white with a softer and less flaky texture. The dough needs to rest in the refrigerator for at least six hours to make the cookies easier to shape, so either prepare it in the morning to bake later in the day or make it the evening before and let it rest overnight to bake the following morning.

Put the butter and confectioners' sugar in a mixing bowl and whisk together until well blended. Add the eggs one at a time, whisking after each addition, and whisk until completely blended. Whisk in the rose water.

Combine the rice flour with the ground cardamom and gradually incorporate into the butter mixture until you have a smooth, firm dough. Cover with plastic wrap and refrigerate for at least 6 hours.

Preheat the oven to 350°F [180°C]. Line a baking sheet with parchment paper or a silicone baking mat.

Use a medium ice-cream scoop or a tablespoon to scoop up a bit of dough the size of an apricot. Roll into a ball and then flatten in your hands, leaving the top rounded. Place on the prepared baking sheet. Use the back of a ½-tsp measure to make an indentation in the middle of the cookie and sprinkle in some poppy seeds. Finish shaping and garnishing the cookies, spacing them 2 to 3 in [5 to 7.5 cm] apart on the sheet.

Bake for 20 minutes. Transfer to a wire rack and let cool. Store in an airtight container at room temperature for up to 1 week.

turkish macaroons

MAKES **24** COOKIES

2 cups [300 g] blanched almonds, plus 24 whole almonds

1½ cups [300 g] superfine sugar

1 tsp almond extract

1 Tbsp freshly squeezed lemon juice

4 egg whites

◆ These are not unlike French *macarons*, though more substantial. They are served on their own without any cream sandwiched in between. If you want them less sweet, grind the almonds with ⅓ cup [65 g] sugar instead of ½ cup [100 g].

Put the blanched almonds in a food processor together with ½ cup [100 g] of the superfine sugar and process until very finely ground. It is very important that you grind the almonds as finely as you can, almost to a powder. Transfer to a large mixing bowl. Add the remaining 1 cup [200 g] sugar, almond extract, lemon juice, and egg whites; mix well.

Scoop the almond mixture into a deep frying pan and place over very low heat. Cook, stirring all the time, for about 20 minutes, until it forms a medium thin paste.

Preheat the oven to 300°F [150°C]. Line a baking sheet with parchment paper or a silicone baking mat.

Transfer the almond paste to a wide bowl, lifting and folding it until cooled. By then, it should have thickened but not become like a dough. Once cool, scoop it into a pastry bag and pipe apricot-size pieces onto the prepared baking sheet, leaving about ½ in [12 mm] between each. Flatten each slightly with the back of a spoon and place one whole almond in the middle of each.

Bake for 20 minutes, then increase the oven temperature to 400°F [200°C] and bake for another 15 minutes. The macaroons should be just golden, not brown; if necessary, lay a sheet of aluminum foil loosely over them. By the time they are done, they should look cracked and just lightly colored. Let cool for a few minutes on the baking sheet, and then transfer to a wire rack to cool completely. Store in an airtight container at room temperature for up to 1 week.

aniseed biscotti

MAKES ABOUT **60** COOKIES

1⅔ cups [250 g] unbleached all-purpose flour

Pinch of fine sea salt

Heaping ½ tsp fast-acting (instant) yeast

¼ tsp aniseed

2 or 3 small grains mastic (see page 55), finely ground in a small mortar with a pestle to yield ⅛ tsp ground mastic (optional)

3 Tbsp organic cane sugar

1½ tsp unsalted butter, at room temperature

1 tsp orange blossom water

¼ cup [60 ml] whole milk

Scant ⅓ cup [80 ml] water

◆ These twice-baked cookies are the Moroccan equivalent of Italian biscotti, made without nuts but with an intriguing combination of aniseed, mastic, and orange blossom water. Even though I indicate the use of mastic as optional, your cookies will benefit from the mysterious flavor it contributes.

Mix the flour, salt, yeast, aniseed, mastic (if using), and sugar in a large mixing bowl. Add the butter, orange blossom water, and milk; mix until you have a crumbly pastry. Gradually add the water (some flours take more water than others) and knead until you have a malleable, firm dough that has the consistency of bread dough. Knead for 3 minutes and shape into a ball. Invert the bowl over it and let rest for 15 minutes. Knead for another 3 minutes until you have a smooth dough—letting it rest facilitates the hydration, and as a result you don't need to knead so vigorously.

Line a large baking sheet with parchment paper or a silicone baking mat.

Pinch off about a third of the dough. Lightly butter your hands and shape the dough into a mini-baguette about 7 in [17 cm] long. Place on the prepared baking sheet. Repeat with each of the remaining thirds; leave about 1 in [2.5 cm] between the three mini-baguettes as they will increase in volume. Cover with a damp, not sopping, kitchen towel and let rise in a warm, draft-free place for 2 hours.

About 20 minutes before the dough is ready, preheat the oven to 400°F [200°C].

Bake the baguettes for 20 to 25 minutes so that they are half-baked. Remove from the oven and let cool. Slice the baguettes crosswise about ½ in [12 mm] thick and lay the cookies flat on two baking sheets, if you have them; otherwise, bake in batches, waiting for the sheet to cool between batches.

Bake again until golden and totally crisp, another 20 minutes. Transfer to a wire rack to cool completely. Store in an airtight container at room temperature for up to 1 week.

sugar-and-spice rings

MAKES ABOUT **40** COOKIES

2 cups [350 g] fine semolina

4 small grains mastic (see page 55), finely ground in a small mortar with a pestle to yield ¼ tsp powdered mastic

⅛ tsp ground nutmeg

Scant ¼ tsp finely ground *mahlab* (see page 20)

⅛ tsp fast-acting (instant) yeast

7½ Tbsp [100 g] unsalted butter, at room temperature

5 Tbsp [75 g] superfine sugar

Scant ½ cup [120 ml] whole milk

◆ When I was a child, I loved to play with these ring-shaped cookies, placing as many as would fit around my fingers before eating them. I have to say I still do this whenever I make them, feeling only a little sheepish about regressing into childhood ways. Muslims make them for the feast of the Sacrifice (Eid al-Adha), which concludes the month of pilgrimage to Mecca known as *Hajj* in Arabic. They are scrumptious and intriguing because they are flavored with both *mahlab* and mastic. Mastic has a mysterious, slightly resiny flavor that can be overwhelming if used in excess. The same can be said of *mahlab*, which when used sparingly imparts subtle nutty and floral flavors. The rings are very simple to make, and their texture is close to shortbread, though a little less crumbly.

Mix the semolina, mastic, nutmeg, *mahlab*, and yeast in a mixing bowl. Add the butter and rub together with the tips of your fingers until the fat is fully incorporated.

Stir the sugar into the milk until it dissolves. Add the sweetened milk to the semolina mixture and knead with your hands until you have a smooth and malleable dough. Cover with a damp, not sopping, kitchen towel and let rest for 1½ hours.

Preheat the oven to 400°F [200°C]. Line two baking sheets with parchment paper or silicone baking mats.

Pinch off a small piece of dough and shape into a ball the size of a small walnut. Roll it into a thin sausage about ½ in [12 mm] thick and 4½ in [11 cm] long. Bring the ends together and lightly press one on top of the other to make a ring about 2 in [5 cm] in diameter. Carefully place on a prepared baking sheet, taking care not to spoil the shape, and continue making and arranging the cookies until you have used up all the dough. You should end up with about 40 cookies.

Bake until golden brown, 15 to 18 minutes. Transfer to a wire rack to cool completely. Store in an airtight container, in a cool place, for up to 2 weeks.

gazelle's horns

MAKES **40** COOKIES

almond filling

3¾ cups [500 g] blanched almonds

¾ cup [150 g] superfine sugar

¼ cup [60 ml] orange blossom water

2 Tbsp unsalted butter, at room temperature

6 to 8 small grains mastic (see page 55), crushed in a small mortar with a pestle to yield ½ tsp powdered mastic

pastry

1½ cups [225 g] unbleached all-purpose flour

2 Tbsp unsalted butter, melted, plus more for rolling out the pastry

6½ Tbsp [100 ml] water

◆ I love these almond-filled cookies. They are baked until just set but not colored so that they remain delicate, breaking as soon as you bite them and then melting in your mouth. I am unable to have a tray of these in front of me without making them disappear with alarming speed.

Even though every self-respecting Moroccan cook knows how to make *cornes de gazelle* (French for "gazelle's horns"— a reference to the cookies' hornlike crescent shape), they are often purchased from specialists, women who bake them to order for both home cooks and pastry shops. A modest *pâtisserie* in Marrakesh was where I found some that were among the best I have ever eaten. Those *cornes de gazelle* were so good that I returned every day to buy some to take to the café next door, to enjoy with my morning mint tea. The waiter disapproved, explaining that the pastries are normally offered at the end of fancy dinner parties known as *diffa* (from *diyafa*, meaning "hospitality" in Arabic), or served throughout the day alongside mint tea. They are not typically eaten for breakfast.

This recipe comes from the Marrakesh woman who made the ones I ate every morning, though I have not been able to roll out the dough as thinly as she did. Nonetheless, my *cornes de gazelle* are delicious and better than any you can buy in commercial North African pastry shops outside the Maghreb.

To make the filling: Put the almonds in a medium heatproof bowl. Pour in enough boiling water to cover and soak for 30 minutes. Drain the almonds and dry them well on a clean kitchen towel.

continued

In a food processor, working in batches if necessary, process the almonds and superfine sugar to a very fine paste, about 2 minutes, scraping down the sides of the bowl as needed. Transfer to a large bowl. Add the orange blossom water, butter, and mastic; mix with your hands until you have a homogeneous paste. Cover with a clean kitchen towel and set aside.

To make the pastry: Put the flour in a large, shallow mixing bowl and make a well in the center. Add the melted butter and slowly add the water (some cooks use orange blossom water, but that makes for very fragrant pastries) as you gradually stir the butter into the flour with your hand or a spatula. Knead the mixture in the bowl for 15 minutes, or until a smooth, malleable dough forms.

Divide the filling into 40 pieces, rolling each piece between the palms of your hands into a 2-in [5-cm] ball. Shape each ball into a cylinder about 4 in [10 cm] long, with tapering ends. Set aside.

Preheat the oven to 400°F [200°C]. Line two baking sheets with parchment paper or silicone baking mats.

Smear your pastry board or work surface, rolling pin, and hands with melted butter. Divide the dough in half and shape each half into a rectangle measuring about 4 by 8 in [10 by 20 cm]. Roll out one half, turning it over once or twice, into a very thin strip about 5 in [12.5 cm] wide and about 20 in [50 cm] long. Carefully stretch the dough with your hands to thin it out a little more and lengthen it to about 25 in [60 cm].

With the dough positioned perpendicular to the counter's edge, place a piece of filling along a short end, about 1 in [2.5 cm] away from the edge. Fold the 1-in [2.5-cm] edge tightly over the filling and pinch the filling, bending it at the same time to form a crescent with a thin triangular body and pointed ends; it should be a little wider than the initial cylinder of filling and flat on the bottom. Press the edges of the dough together and cut using a fluted pastry wheel, following the shape of the crescent and keeping very close to the edge of the filling. The crescent should measure about 4 in [10 cm] wide by 1¼ in [3 cm] high. Prick it with a toothpick in several places on both sides and set on a prepared baking sheet. Form more *cornes de gazelle* in the same way using the rolled-out dough; you should have enough to make 20 crescents. Space them about 1 in [2.5 cm] apart on the baking sheet.

Bake until barely colored, 15 to 20 minutes. Let the pastries cool a little, and then carefully transfer them to a wire rack to cool completely. While the first batch is baking, begin forming the second lot, and bake and cool them in the same way. Store in an airtight container at room temperature for up to 5 days.

rose water and orange blossom water

These fragrant waters are distilled from the macerated blossoms of the Damascus rose (*ward jouri* in Arabic) and the Seville orange (*bou-sfayr*). Used extensively in Levantine desserts, both rose water and orange blossom water are distilled with the help of an alembic.

Rose water can be used fairly freely—that is, if you don't mind flavors that remind you of perfume. Orange blossom water, on the other hand, needs to be used sparingly because it can become bitter and/or overwhelming when used in excess. The two waters are often combined and used in syrups as well as in many sweets, including milk puddings and ice cream.

Orange blossom water is also used in a tisane as a delicate, aromatic substitute for real coffee, and is called white coffee (*qahwa bayda*). To make it, add 1 tsp of orange blossom water to a small cup of boiling water.

Keep in mind that not all fragrant waters are equal, and unless you can buy homemade ones as I do in Lebanon, I recommend buying a good commercial brand like Mymoune, which produces the fragrant waters artisanally.

frozen
desserts

mango sorbet

MAKES ABOUT **1** QT [**1** L]

½ cup [100 g] organic cane sugar

¼ tsp freshly squeezed lemon juice

¾ cup [180 ml] water

4¼ lb [2 kg] ripe mangoes, preferably Alphonso, peeled and pitted

◆ The word *sorbet* comes from the Arabic word *sharbat*, meaning "drinks." Most commercial sorbets have egg white added to them but I like the purity of this one, where nothing apart from the sugar syrup interferes with the intense taste of the mangoes. My favorite mangoes are Alphonsos from India. They are very sweet and not at all stringy.

Put the sugar, lemon juice, and ¼ cup [60 ml] of the water in a small saucepan and place over medium heat. Bring to a boil, stirring occasionally, and let bubble for 5 minutes. Remove from the heat and let cool.

Put the mango pulp and cooled syrup in a food processor. Add the remaining water and process until completely creamy. Transfer to a 2-qt [2-L] measuring cup. Cover with plastic wrap and refrigerate for a couple of hours, until thoroughly chilled.

Transfer to an ice-cream maker and process according to the manufacturer's instructions. Transfer to an airtight container and put in the freezer; leave uncovered for the first 10 minutes of freezing to avoid the formation of ice crystals. Store, covered, in the freezer for up to 1 month.

fig ice cream

MAKES ABOUT **1¼** QT [**1.25** L]

1¼ cups [300 ml] whole milk

18 oz [500 g] fresh ripe figs

**1¼ cups [300 ml] crème
fraîche**

**¾ cup plus 2 Tbsp [175 g]
superfine sugar**

◆ The color of this ice cream will vary according to the type of figs you use. I like to use purple figs, for their vibrant color. I also find their flavor stronger than that of the sweeter and more subtle green figs. That said, all types are suitable as long as the figs are ripe and sweet. You can use this recipe as the base recipe for any other fruit ice cream, varying it endlessly by using whatever fruit is in season, from mulberries to mangoes to strawberries to prickly pears to bananas. The only thing to change is the amount of sugar, according to the sweetness of the fruit. If you are using berries, cook them lightly with the sugar before pulping them to get rid of some of their water content. I was given this very useful tip by Shuna Lydon, pastry chef extraordinaire, who worked at the French Laundry, among many other places.

Put the milk in a saucepan, place over medium heat, and bring to a boil. Watch carefully so the milk doesn't boil over. Remove from the heat and let cool.

Process the figs in a food processor until reduced to a mush. Transfer the puréed figs to a mixing bowl with a spout or a large measuring cup. Strain the cooled milk over them and add the crème fraîche and sugar. Stir until the sugar has dissolved and the cream is fully incorporated. Cover with plastic wrap and refrigerate for a couple of hours, until thoroughly chilled.

Transfer to an ice-cream maker and process according to the manufacturer's instructions. Transfer to an airtight container and put in the freezer; leave uncovered for the first 10 minutes of freezing to avoid the formation of ice crystals. Store, covered, in the freezer for up to 1 month.

FROZEN DESSERTS

date
ice cream

MAKES **1½** QT [**1.5** L]

¼ cup [40 g] cornstarch

4 cups [960 ml] goat's milk

½ cup [100 g] organic cane
    sugar

Pinch of saffron threads

2 Tbsp rose water

2 tsp ground cardamom

**3 cups [450 g] pitted dates,
preferably Khlass**

**1 cup [240 ml] goat's cream
or crème fraîche**

**3 Tbsp slivered or chopped
pistachios**

**1 Tbsp dried unsprayed
rose petals**

◆ This is a luscious ice cream, flecked with brown bits of date that you can strain out if you want the ice cream to be totally silky. I love the combination of saffron, cardamom, and rose water—the quintessential flavors of the Arabian Gulf, in both savory and sweet dishes. I often use goat's milk and goat's cream in my ice creams because the results are lighter and more flavorful, but you don't need to follow my example if these ingredients are unavailable. Substitute a very good organic whole milk and crème fraîche. The ideal dates to use here are Khlass from Saudi Arabia, but these may not be readily available, so substitute Deglet Noor, Barhi, or Medjool if you need to.

Whisk the cornstarch into ½ cup [120 ml] of the goat's milk.

Put the remaining goat's milk, the sugar, and saffron in a saucepan and place over medium heat. Slowly add the cornstarch-milk mixture, whisking all the time. Bring to a boil, still whisking. Let bubble for about 5 minutes while still whisking, until the milk has thickened and taken on a pale yellow color from the saffron. Remove from the heat and add the rose water and cardamom. Cover with a clean kitchen towel and let cool.

Put the dates and goat's cream in a food processor—even if you buy pitted dates, check them for pits. Process until the dates are pulverized. Add about 1 cup [240 ml] of the thickened milk and process until the mixture is creamy. Transfer to a 2-qt [2-L] measuring cup and add the remaining thickened milk. Whisk until well blended. Cover with plastic wrap and refrigerate for a couple of hours, until the mixture is thoroughly chilled.

Transfer the mixture to an ice-cream maker and process according to the manufacturer's instructions. Transfer to an airtight container and put in the freezer; leave the container uncovered for the first 10 minutes of freezing to avoid the formation of ice crystals. Store, covered, in the freezer for up to 1 month. Serve sprinkled with the pistachios and dried rose petals.

apricot leather ice cream

MAKES ABOUT **1¼** QT [**1.25** L]

⅓ cup [50 g] pine nuts

10 oz [300 g] apricot leather (see facing page)

2 cups [480 ml] whole milk

1 cup [240 ml] crème fraîche

½ cup [100 g] superfine sugar (optional)

¼ cup [60 ml] orange blossom water

◆ *Qamar al-din*, which means "moon of the religion," is the Arabic name for apricot leather, though I do not know how it got such a poetic name. This ice cream is a classic Lebanese concoction that I first discovered in a Lebanese cookbook written by Ibrahim Mouzannar. I then tasted it at the Beirut shop of the late Hanna Mitri, Lebanon's ice-cream maker extraordinaire. The shop is still going strong, manned by his son, who inherited Hanna's secret formulas. The following recipe is not his but rather adapted from Mouzannar's book *Cuisine Libanaise*. Hanna was notoriously secretive about his formulas and never shared them with anyone apart from his son.

Place the pine nuts in a small bowl and pour over enough water to cover. Let sit for 1 hour.

Meanwhile, cut the apricot leather into medium-size pieces and put in a saucepan.

Add the milk to the pan and place over medium-low heat. Stir every now and then until the apricot leather has completely melted. Toward the end of cooking, use a whisk to facilitate the disintegration process, which will take 20 to 30 minutes. Do not leave the pan unattended for more than a few minutes; the milk may curdle if it is allowed to boil. Transfer to a 2-qt [2-L] measuring cup and add the crème fraîche. Whisk until well blended. Taste before adding the sugar, in case you find the mixture sweet enough already. Remember, though, that when the mixture freezes, the taste will become less sweet—in fact, freezing dulls all flavors. Add as much of the sugar as you wish, together with the orange blossom water; whisk until the sugar has completely dissolved.

Drain the pine nuts, rinse under cold water, and add to the apricot leather mixture. Stir to combine well. Cover with plastic wrap and refrigerate for a couple of hours, until thoroughly chilled.

Transfer the mixture to an ice-cream maker and process according to the manufacturer's instructions. Transfer to an airtight container and put in the freezer; leave the container uncovered for the first 10 minutes of freezing to avoid the formation of ice crystals. Store, covered, in the freezer for up to 1 month.

apricot leather

As much as I loved Pierrot caramel lollipops when I was a child—I still do, by the way—I loved sucking on torn sheets of apricot leather even more. And whenever I use apricot leather to make a drink or a sweet juice or ice cream, I still tear off a piece to suck on the way I did as a child. Apricot leather is made by pulping fresh apricots at the height of the season and cooking the pulp with sugar before spreading it thickly and letting it dry. It is one way to preserve apricots, whose season is so lamentably short. There are different brands, some sweeter than others, so taste a little before using so that you can adjust the sugar. One of my favorites is Sofra; look for it in Middle Eastern markets. If you cannot find it, any good-quality apricot leather will work.

rose water and mastic ice cream

MAKES ABOUT **1¼** QT [**1.25** L]

4 cups [960 ml] whole milk

8 grains mastic (see page 55), finely ground in a small mortar with a pestle to yield ½ tsp powdered mastic

1 Tbsp salep or ¼ cup [40 g] cornstarch

¾ cup [150 g] superfine sugar

1¼ cups [300 ml] crème fraîche

2 Tbsp rose water

2 Tbsp slivered or chopped pistachios, or a few unsprayed dried rose petals for garnish (optional)

◆ Middle Eastern ice cream is denser than Western ice cream because it is thickened not with eggs but with salep, a mysterious ingredient ground from dried wild orchid tubers (see facing page). You can use cornstarch instead of salep but you won't get the same luscious, chewy texture typical of salep ice cream. If you can, get a pure salep; it will be grayish, with speckles. But you can also use a commercial salep mix. If you opt for the salep mix, increase the amount specified in the recipe by one-quarter. You can substitute 1 Tbsp orange blossom water or a vanilla bean for the rose water (see Variation).

In a small bowl, stir together 2 Tbsp of the milk and the mastic.

If you are using salep, put the remaining milk in a saucepan and place over medium heat. Bring the milk to a boil and add the salep gradually, in very small quantities, whisking vigorously without stopping (this is to prevent clots from forming in the milk). Keep whisking over the heat for about 10 minutes, until the milk has thickened. If using cornstarch, dilute it in ½ cup [120 ml] milk, and whisk the cornstarch mixture into the remaining milk as soon as you put it on the heat; continue whisking until it has boiled for about 5 minutes.

Add the sugar to the milk mixture and stir for 1 minute or so, until the sugar has completely dissolved. Remove from the heat.

Add the crème fraîche and rose water to the mixture and stir well. Add the mastic-milk and mix well. Let cool, cover with plastic wrap, and refrigerate for a couple of hours, until thoroughly chilled.

Transfer the mixture to an ice-cream maker and process according to the manufacturer's instructions. Transfer to an airtight container and put in the freezer; leave the container uncovered for the first 10 minutes of freezing to avoid the formation of ice crystals. Store, covered, in the freezer for up to 1 month. Serve garnished with pistachios or dried rose petals, if desired.

Variation: Instead of the rose water, you can use a vanilla bean, added at the start. Split the bean lengthwise and scrape the seeds into the milk before heating.

SAHLAB
salep

Salep (*sahlab* in Arabic) is produced from the tubers of *Orchis mascula* or *O. militaris*, which are dried and ground to produce a very fine, slightly grayish flour. But be warned, not all saleps are equal. Because it is both rare and expensive, some vendors cheat and mix salep with cornstarch. Pure salep is now difficult to find outside the Middle East—in fact, there is an export ban on it in Turkey—but you can use salep mix with good results. This is readily available in Middle Eastern stores. If you do opt for a salep mix, increase the amount specified in the recipe by 25 percent.

Salep thickens the ice cream, giving it a stretchy, chewy consistency that prolongs the pleasure of eating it. In addition, the ice cream is either churned to incorporate less air or, as is done in Syria, frozen against the walls of the ice-cream maker and then beaten, resulting in ice cream with no air in it at all.

saffron ice cream

MAKES ABOUT ¾ QT [**720** ML]

2 Tbsp cornstarch

2 cups [480 ml] whole milk

Good pinch of saffron threads

Pinch of sea salt

¾ cup [150 g] organic cane sugar

½ cup [120 ml] crème fraîche

1 tsp rose water

⅓ cup [50 g] slivered or chopped pistachios

◆ It is becoming more difficult to find real saffron ice cream in Iran these days. Either it is not made with true saffron or it doesn't have frozen shards of cream inside. I love this ice cream with its heady flavor and exquisite color, but when I make it, I skip the frozen cream shards as they are fairly troublesome to produce, especially if you don't have much free space in your freezer. Instead, I garnish with pistachios for a lovely contrast between their vivid green color and the pale yellow hue from the saffron. It is difficult to find salep in the United States, so I have replaced it with cornstarch. If you have some salep, use 1½ tsp in place of the cornstarch.

Whisk the cornstarch into ½ cup [120 ml] of the milk.

Put the remaining milk in a saucepan and add the saffron and salt. Let the saffron infuse in the milk for 30 minutes.

Put the saffron-milk over medium-high heat and whisk the cornstarch-milk into it. Keep whisking until the milk comes to a boil, at which point it will start to thicken. Turn the heat to medium-low. Add the sugar and continue whisking for another 10 minutes.

Take the milk off the heat and pour into a 2-qt [2-L] measuring cup. Whisk in the crème fraîche and rose water. Cover with a clean kitchen towel and let cool. Whisk the milk regularly at first to prevent a skin from forming. Let cool completely, cover with plastic wrap, and refrigerate for a couple of hours, until thoroughly chilled.

continued

Transfer to an ice-cream maker and process according to the manufacturer's instructions. Transfer to an airtight container and put in the freezer; leave the container uncovered for the first 10 minutes of freezing to avoid the formation of ice crystals. Store, covered, in the freezer for up to 1 month. Serve sprinkled with the pistachios.

persian sweet noodles

SERVES **4** TO **6**

3 cups [720 ml] water
1 cup [125 g] cornstarch

◆ This interesting ancient Persian preparation is very simple to make. According to Margaret Shaida, whose recipe I have adapted here from her brilliant book, *The Legendary Cuisine of Persia*, it used to be made in droplike grains the size of rice and served with fruit syrups. Perhaps it is the precursor of tapioca, though the brittle texture is different. The taste of *paludeh* really depends on what you serve it with. On its own, it has no flavor, but the noodles come alive as soon as you serve them over ice cream such as the Saffron Ice Cream (page 118). You can also serve them over a granita made with your choice of fruit syrup. Pomegranate, mulberry, or rose would be appropriate Persian flavors. This refreshing dish is unusual and very pretty, and it's definitely worth trying.

Prepare a bowl of ice water into which you will pipe the *paludeh* to both cool and shape it.

Put 1 cup [240 ml] of the water in a saucepan and whisk in the cornstarch. Gradually add the remaining 2 cups [480 ml] water, whisking all the time. Place the pan over medium heat and bring to a boil, still whisking. You do not want the mixture to be lumpy. Continue whisking until you have a thick white paste that is very smooth, about 2 minutes.

Let the paste cool a little before transferring it to a pastry bag fitted with a very fine nozzle, the finest you have. Pipe the paste into the ice water to create a tangle of thin noodles, working quickly so the paste stays pliable; the noodles should stay in the ice water for no more than 5 minutes. Drain before serving.

FROZEN DESSERTS

halva ice cream

MAKES ABOUT **1½** QT [**1.5** L]

¼ cup [40 g] cornstarch

4 cups [960 ml] goat's milk or whole milk

½ cup [100 g] organic cane sugar

2 Tbsp rose water

1 tsp ground cardamom

17 oz [500 g] tahini halva, finely crumbled

1 cup [240 ml] goat's cream or crème fraîche

3 Tbsp slivered or chopped pistachios

◆ A long time ago a Turkish friend, Hande Bozdoğan, who owns and runs the Istanbul Culinary Institute, gave me a recipe for tahini ice cream that I lost. I could have asked her to send it again, but before I could do so I found this interesting recipe for halva ice cream in Afnan Rashid al-Zayani's book, *A Taste of the Arabian Gulf*, and decided to adapt it. It is a little sweeter than Hande's recipe but with an interesting texture, half creamy and half crunchy—or as crunchy as an ice cream can be. It is definitely worth trying, and you can vary the flavor by adding saffron to the milk or replacing the cardamom with white pepper, for an intriguing spicy taste. If you opt for the pepper, use ½ tsp.

Whisk the cornstarch into ½ cup [120 ml] of the milk.

Put the remaining milk and the sugar in a saucepan and place over medium heat. Slowly add the cornstarch-milk, whisking all the time. Bring to a boil, still whisking. Let bubble for about 5 minutes, continuing to whisk, until the milk has thickened. Remove from the heat and add the rose water and cardamom. Cover with a clean kitchen towel and let cool.

Put the crumbled halva and goat's cream in a food processor and process to a smooth paste. If the mixture is too thick, add 1 cup [240 ml] of the thickened milk and process until the mixture is creamy. Transfer to a 2-qt [2-L] measuring cup. Add the thickened milk and whisk until well blended. Cover with plastic wrap and refrigerate for a couple of hours, until thoroughly chilled.

Transfer to an ice-cream maker and process according to the manufacturer's instructions. Transfer to an airtight container and put in the freezer; leave the container uncovered for the first 10 minutes of freezing to avoid the formation of ice crystals. Store, covered, in the freezer for up to 1 month. Serve sprinkled with the pistachios.

jams
and
confections

citron jelly

MAKES **6** CUPS [**1.9** KG]

2¾ lb [1.3 kg] citrons

4 cups [800 g] organic cane sugar

◆ Citron, known as *cédrat* in French and *cedro* in Italian, resembles a very large lemon. In ancient times, the fruit was known as Persian apple because the Romans thought it originated in Persia. Under the citron's knobby yellow skin is a very thick white pith, which is the main attraction of the fruit rather than its dry pulp. In Sicily, the rind is candied and used in sweets. In Iran and Pakistan, the rind is made into jam, while in India it is pickled.

This unusual Tunisian confection needs to be eaten within a couple of weeks of making it. It has no hint of bitterness and is delightful served with cottage cheese, other fresh white cheese, or yogurt. I have adapted this recipe from Zeinab Kaak's book *La Sofra: Cuisine Tunisienne Traditionelle*. Use three 1-pt [480-ml] sterilized jars (see page 129), and be sure to allow plenty of time for soaking the citrons.

Soak the citrons in enough water to cover for 2 days, changing the water each day.

Peel the citrons, removing only the outer yellow layer, and discard the skin (or slice it in thin strips, dry, and use in other recipes). Remove the white pith and grate it finely. Discard the citron pulp. Put the grated pith in a medium saucepan and add 2½ cups [600 ml] water. Place the pan over medium heat and bring to a boil. Lower the heat and let simmer for about 30 minutes.

Add the sugar and bring back to a boil; lower the heat again and simmer for 25 to 30 minutes. Remove from the heat, cover the pan with a clean kitchen towel, and let cool. Pour the jelly into sterilized jam jars. Seal the jars and refrigerate. Store in the refrigerator for up to 2 weeks.

orange blossom jam

MAKES **1** PT [**640** ML]

2¼ lb [1 kg] orange blossoms

4 cups [800 g] organic cane sugar

A few drops of natural red food coloring

½ cup [120 ml] freshly squeezed lemon juice

◆ Orange blossoms have a special place in Middle Eastern kitchens, both the fragrant water distilled from the flowers and the jam made with them. It is easier to make the jam at home than to distill the water, a job for which you need a special still. In the Middle East, it is easy to buy the blossoms when in season. I tested this recipe with my friend Amy Dencler, who cooks at Chez Panisse, picking the blossoms on Mary Taylor Simeti's farm in Sicily in spring. If you live in California or Florida, you will be able to get the blossoms, and I promise it is well worth your while to do so. This jam is incredibly beautiful, the blossoms turning a pastel pink because of the added natural colorant. Middle Eastern sweets makers use enough artificial coloring to turn the blossoms red, and then use them as a garnish on creamy sweets; the blossoms have a delightful and subtle floral flavor. The only drawback is that it takes a fairly long time to pick the petals off the flowers. Orange blossom jam is also available commercially but it lacks the purity of homemade. Use two ½-pt [240-ml] sterilized jars (see facing page).

Pick the petals off the orange blossoms. Place in a medium saucepan with enough water to cover them by about ¾ in [2 cm]. Bring to a boil and continue boiling for 30 minutes. Drain and rinse under cold water; let them soak in a bowl of fresh water while you make the syrup.

Put the sugar in a saucepan. Add 1½ qt [1.5 L] water and bring to a boil. Add the food coloring and simmer for 30 minutes; let cool.

Drain the blossoms well and add to the syrup. Let soak for 24 hours. Strain the blossoms out of the syrup, return the syrup to the saucepan, and boil the syrup for another 10 minutes. Return the blossoms to the syrup and let bubble for 10 minutes longer, then add the lemon juice. Let bubble for a final 10 minutes.

Pour the jam into sterilized jam jars. Cover each jar with a piece of wax paper, immediately seal the jars, and let cool. Store in the refrigerator for up to 3 months.

how to sterilize jars for jam

I sterilize jars in the oven. Wash them well in soapy water, rinse, and dry them before standing them on a baking sheet. Put the baking sheet in a cold oven and turn the oven to 275°F [140°C]. Let the jars sit in the oven for 30 minutes. Turn off the oven and let the jars cool in the oven before using them. Alternatively, you can run the jars through the dishwasher—make sure the drying function is on.

barberry jam

MAKES **3** CUPS [**960** G]

1²⁄₃ cups [250 g] dried
barberries, rinsed

2 cups [480 ml] apple juice

1 cinnamon stick

4 green cardamom pods

Pinch of saffron threads

1 cup [200 g] organic cane
sugar

◆ All over the Middle East and North Africa, people spend much of the end of summer preserving surplus produce. They dry or pickle vegetables, and they candy fruit or make jams with them. Each country has a local jam made with a typically local fruit, and this barberry jam is made with one of Iran's essential ingredients, barberries (*zereshk*, in Persian). Too sour to eat raw, barberries were used in England in medieval times to add an astringent note to quince and other bland fruits. They remained fairly sought after at the beginning of the twentieth century. The barberry bush was extirpated in England once it was found to harbor wheat-mildew parasites. In Iran, barberries are used mainly in savory dishes such as *zereshk polow* (barberry pilaf) and *morasa polow* (jeweled rice).

I have bought dark-colored barberries and I have bought them in vivid red. The more vibrant the color, the prettier the jam, but the sweet-sour taste will be pretty much the same. If you can't find barberries, you can substitute dried sour cherries. Use three ½-pt [240-ml] sterilized jars (see page 129). Start this recipe the night before you plan to cook the jam.

Put the rinsed barberries in a bowl. Pour the apple juice over them and cover with plastic wrap. Place the bowl in the refrigerator to soak overnight.

Put the barberries and apple juice in a large saucepan—you don't want the mixture to boil over during cooking. Add the cinnamon stick, cardamom pods, and saffron and place over high heat. Bring to a boil, stirring constantly. Slowly add the sugar, still stirring. Let bubble for 4 minutes, always stirring. Remove from the heat and discard the cinnamon stick.

Pour the jam into sterilized jam jars. Cover each jar with wax paper, immediately seal the jars, and let cool. Store in the refrigerator for up to 3 months.

sweet almond and argan oil spread

MAKES **1** PT [**500** G]

Heaping 1⅓ cups [200 g] unpeeled almonds, toasted (see page 25)

½ cup [120 ml] argan oil

¼ cup [60 g] good-quality honey, warmed

Pinch of sea salt

◆ Argan oil is no longer difficult to find, though it is still expensive. Nonetheless, it is worth using here because it has a delightful, subtle nutty taste, and its texture is lighter than other oils. It is a little like walnut oil but with a more distinctive flavor. The fruit of the argan tree is eaten by goats or camels, who chew on the pulp and then process the kernels the natural way, expelling them all over the ground around the trees. Locals, mostly women, scour the ground to find the kernels, which they collect, wash, and crack to reveal the nuts inside. They roast the nuts and send them to be pressed for the oil. If you are buying the oil in Morocco, beware the fake ones and buy your oil from a reliable source. I was once sold a whole bottle that was nothing but colored vegetable oil.

Amlou is a thick paste made with nuts and argan oil. It is said to have such healthful properties as restoring strength to new mothers and virility to old men. I like it because of its sweet, nutty flavor and smooth texture—a kind of superior and sweet peanut butter. Serve *amlou* with good bread or crackers for breakfast or afternoon tea.

Process the almonds in a food processor until finely ground. With the machine running, add the argan oil slowly, as you would add the oil when making a mayonnaise. If you have speeds on your processor, do this on a low speed so as not to heat up the oil. Once the oil is fully incorporated, transfer to a bowl and mix in the warmed honey—warming makes it less thick—and salt. Store, covered, in a cool place or in the refrigerator for up to 1 month.

sugared almonds

SERVES **6** TO **8**

3⅓ cups [500 g] blanched almonds

2½ cups [500 g] organic cane sugar

¾ cup [180 ml] water

1 tsp ground cardamom

◆ Although your results might not be as perfect as the professionals', it is fun to know how some of these Arabian sweets are made and rewarding to make them. Be careful here how long you cook the syrup, and do not slack off when shaking the nuts in the pan with the syrup. Both are essential for good results. As a child, I also loved sugared roasted chickpeas (see Variation).

Preheat the oven to 400°F [200°C].

Spread the almonds on a baking sheet and toast in the oven for 6 to 8 minutes.

Put the sugar and water in a saucepan. Add the cardamom and place over medium heat. Bring to a boil and let simmer for 2 minutes, until the syrup thickens slightly.

Put half the toasted almonds in a large frying pan and place over low heat. Pour the syrup, 1 Tbsp at a time, over the nuts; after each addition, shake the almonds to coat them evenly. Starting halfway through, you will need to stir the nuts with a spoon, as simply shaking the pan may not move them so easily. By the time you've added half the syrup, the almonds should be completely white. Transfer to a serving bowl or a container and repeat the process with the remaining almonds and syrup. Store in an airtight container at room temperature for up to 2 weeks.

Variation: To make sugared chickpeas, buy roasted, unsalted chickpeas from a Middle Eastern shop and substitute them for the almonds.

candied green walnuts

SERVES **6** TO **8**

¼ cup [40 g] slaked lime

2 lb [910 g] green walnuts, picked when still quite young

5 cups [1 kg] organic cane sugar

◆   There is a wonderful tradition in the Middle East of keeping bowls of sweets to offer guests as soon as coffee or tea is served. They range from simple crunchy sugared almonds to such chewy confections as Syrian *malban* (the Arab equivalent of Turkish delight, studded with nuts), made with grape juice. Candied fruit is also kept on the coffee table, but in separate bowls and under a lid to keep them from drying out. The Syrian ones are the best—a specialty of Damascus—and the selection includes the whole range of fruit as well as such delicacies as green walnuts and baby eggplant. Each candied fruit, nut, or vegetable is nestled into its own little paper cup and, depending on how elegant the maker, they are arranged in beautiful boxes or simply slipped into plastic. I always bought more candied walnuts than anything else because I like the firm skin and the soft crunch of the tender shell. I give a recipe for making these even though they are not so easily done at home. For centuries, Middle Eastern home cooks and sweets makers alike treat the green nuts with calcium hydroxide, also known as slaked lime, "Cal," pickling lime, or lime paste. In Arabic it is known as *kilss*, meaning "chalk," and it is used as a firming agent by diluting it in water and letting the fruit or vegetables soak in it overnight.

Dissolve the slaked lime in 2 qt [2 L] water. Peel the walnuts with a vegetable peeler, removing only a thin coat of skin, and put the nuts to soak in the lime water for 24 hours.

Heat a saucepan of water to the boiling point. Rinse the walnuts and blanch them in the boiling water for just a minute or two. Drain and set aside.

Put the sugar in a saucepan. Add 1 cup [240 ml] water and place over medium heat. Bring to a boil and let the syrup simmer for a few minutes. Then drop in the walnuts and simmer for 20 to 25 minutes. You can leave them in the syrup as the Turks and Greeks do, or you can take them out to drain on a wire rack placed over a baking sheet for 1 hour or so. Store in individual paper cups in an airtight container at room temperature for up to 3 weeks.

buttery walnut-stuffed dates

SERVES **6** TO **8**

¾ cup [100 g] walnut halves, broken in half lengthwise

1 Tbsp slivered almonds

3 cups [450 g] Iranian, Deglet Noor, Barhi, or Medjool dates

1 cup [220 g] unsalted butter

1⅔ cups [250 g] unbleached all-purpose flour

2 Tbsp confectioners' sugar

1 Tbsp slivered or chopped pistachios

◆ This truly delectable dessert features textural contrasts, with the crunchy toasted walnuts coming as a lovely surprise as you bite into the soft, melting dates. Iranian dates are some of the best you can buy. If you can find them, by all means use them; otherwise use Deglet Noor, Barhi, or Medjool dates. *Ranginak* means "colorful" in Persian, and this dessert lives up to the name because of the slivers of green pistachios and golden toasted almonds that are scattered all over the top. Serve these dates as a sweet snack with tea, Turkish coffee, or the drink of your choice, or as a dessert at the end of a meal. According to the late Margaret Shaida, author of the magisterial volume *The Legendary Cuisine of Persia*, whose recipe I have adapted here, *ranginak* was served in the imperial court in seventeenth-century Isfahan, covered with a layer of creamy rice pudding before the nuts were sprinkled all over.

Preheat the oven to 450°F [220°C].

Spread the walnut quarters and the slivered almonds over two separate baking sheets and toast in the oven until lightly colored, 3 to 5 minutes. Check on the almonds after 3 minutes in case they are coloring too fast. Take the nuts out of the oven and let cool.

Make a slit down the middle of each date, but only on one side, and, with the tip of the knife, gently pry open to slide the pit out. Insert a walnut quarter inside each date, again being very careful. Press on the ends to close each date and lay them neatly on a serving dish, leaving about ¼ in [6 mm] between each.

Melt the butter in a large skillet over medium heat and stir in the flour and confectioners' sugar. Keep stirring over the heat until the mixture turns golden. Pour the mixture between the dates, filling the gaps; if there is any butter mixture left, pour it over the dates. Let the dates sit for about 1 hour, and then sprinkle with the pistachios and toasted almonds. Store in an airtight container at room temperature for up to 1 day.

dates

Long before oil, Gulf Arabs had dates. Dates were a staple—their main sustenance, together with bread and milk—until oil riches changed their lives and, as a result, their diet. Dates were also an edible commodity used as barter with neighboring tribes. Dates have been central to people's diet in the region since the earliest period of the Egyptian and Mesopotamian civilizations, and actual dates were found in tombs of all epochs from the fifth dynasty (2494 to 2345 B.C.) onward. The date palm has been used extensively throughout history as a decorative element in art and architecture.

It is not easy to pinpoint the exact location of the first date palms. According to one narrative, the tree was first planted in Medina by the descendants of Noah after the Flood. If it wasn't Medina, it was in an equally hot place with plenty of water; as the Arabs say, "The date palm needs its feet in water and its head in the fire of the sky." It is therefore probable that the date palm first appeared in the oases of the Arabian desert. It is still where most date palms are grown, with Saudi Arabia being the world's second-largest grower after Iraq. The date palm is also grown on the coasts of Africa, in southern Spain, in western Asia, and in California. The soldiers of Alexander the Great are said to have introduced it to northern India, spitting the stones from their date rations around the camp so that, in the course of time, palm groves grew there.

There are three main types of date: soft, hard, and semidry. The semidry is most popular in the West. Soft dates are grown in the Middle East mainly to eat fresh, though they are also dried and compressed into blocks to be used in a range of sweets, including the date-filled pastries on page 60. As for hard dates, also called camel dates, they are dry and fibrous even when fresh. When dried, they become extremely hard and sweet and keep for years.

Dates still play an important role in the diet of Gulf Arabs, if no longer as a staple. They are the first thing people eat when they break the long day's fast during the month of Ramadan. Their high sugar content, up to 70 percent by weight in a fully dried date, makes them an ideal way to break the fast after so many hours without any food or water, supplying the necessary rush of energy while easy on an empty stomach. Some people eat them plain, others dip them in tahini, and others have them with yogurt, cheese, or a kind of fresh cheese curd called *yiğit*. Dates also feature prominently, both in savory and sweet dishes. Date syrup is also used to make a drink called *jallab*, which is sold on the street, packed with crushed ice and garnished with pine nuts and golden raisins.

persian marzipan "mulberries"

MAKES ABOUT **70** PIECES

3¼ cups [260 g] almond meal

1 tsp ground cardamom

2 cups [260 g] confectioners' sugar

3 Tbsp rose water

Superfine sugar for rolling

3 Tbsp slivered pistachios

◆ This Persian marzipan is made exotic by the rose water and cardamom, and made attractive by shaping it like mulberries and inserting a sliver of pistachio at the top of the fruit to make it look like a stalk. (For those unfamiliar with mulberries, the fruits resemble elongated blackberries.) You can shape the marzipan any way you want, and make it look like other fruits or even paint it as they do in Sicily, though if you do this, be sure to use natural dyes. These make delightful host or hostess gifts, especially if you find a pretty box to arrange them in.

Put the almond meal, cardamom, and confectioners' sugar in a mixing bowl. Mix well; add the rose water, 1 Tbsp at a time, kneading it into the almond mixture until you have a malleable dough.

Spread a little superfine sugar on a plate. Pinch off about 1 tsp of marzipan and shape like a mulberry. Repeat, shaping half the marzipan. Roll the "mulberries" in the sugar to coat them evenly. Stick a pistachio sliver in the top of each to make it look like a stalk. Shape the remaining marzipan to make another batch. Store in an airtight container at room temperature for up to 3 days.

omani "jellies"

SERVES **4** TO **6**

Good pinch of saffron threads

2 tsp rose water

3 Tbsp cornstarch

2 cups [480 ml] water

½ tsp ground cardamom

¾ cup plus 2 Tbsp [175 g] superfine sugar

4 Tbsp [55 g] unsalted butter

1 Tbsp slivered or chopped pistachios

◆ Called *Masghati* because it is a specialty of Muscat, Oman, this is a typical hospitality sweet automatically served in the United Arab Emirates to visitors for both small and important occasions. I remember one extraordinary wedding in an encampment in the arid mountains above al-'Ayn, an emirate near Abu Dhabi. There was a large tent with cushions lined up against the tent walls for the guests to sit on. And in front of the cushions were placed large platters of rice with roasted baby goats. These were arranged at regular intervals to feed every six to eight guests. Right by the platters were little plastic containers filled with Omani "jellies" for guests to enjoy after the meal. I couldn't quite see how to scoop the wobbly sweet with my fingers without making them all sticky, so I ended up not eating any. Our host must have noticed because he insisted I take some with me as we prepared to leave. The making of this sweet is quite similar to Turkish delight (*rahat lokum*) in that it is simply water thickened with cornstarch, but in this case the flavoring is cardamom, saffron, and rose water. The luxurious version has nuts added to it. Serve *Masghati* with tea, coffee, or a tisane at the end of a meal or at any other time when you feel like having a sweet snack.

Butter a medium shallow serving bowl. Put the saffron threads to soak in the rose water and let infuse for a few minutes.

In a medium saucepan, stir the cornstarch into the water. Add the cardamom, sugar, and butter; place over medium heat, stirring constantly, until the mixture comes to a boil and starts thickening. Continue stirring for a few minutes more and then remove from the heat; stir in the saffron–rose water mixture. Pour the mixture into the prepared serving bowl. Let cool before sprinkling the pistachios all over. Store in an airtight container at room temperature for up to 1 week. To serve, spoon into bowls.

saffron-caramel
wafers

MAKES **16** PIECES

Pinch of saffron threads
¼ cup [60 ml] water
1 cup [200 g] superfine sugar
Pinch of sea salt

◆ Iranians, like many Eastern Europeans, sip tea through sugar cubes so that it sweetens as they drink it. I also like to sweeten my tea this way, though I go wild for the version I discovered in the Abbasi Hotel in Isfahan, where people sweeten their tea with diaphanous saffron-caramel wafers, so thin you can read through them. You can't read through my 2.5-mm wafers, though they are delightful to hold in your mouth as you let the tea melt them a little with each sip.

Place the saffron threads in a bowl and pour the water over. Let sit for about 30 minutes to infuse.

Stir together the sugar, saffron water, and salt in a small saucepan and place over medium-high heat. Stop stirring and let the sugar start to melt and turn light golden, about 3 minutes. Continue cooking, stirring occasionally, until the sugar has completely melted and has turned a slightly darker golden color. This should take 5 to 7 minutes longer.

Have a silicone baking mat ready and very quickly drop small, thin circles, about 1 in [2.5 cm] in diameter, of caramel onto the mat. You need to work very quickly, as the caramel will harden in no time. Let set until completely dry and crisp, 20 to 30 minutes. If you want the wafers to be really thin, place another silicone mat over them and quickly press on it with a rolling pin, rolling back and forth until the wafers have spread very thinly. Store in an airtight container at room temperature for up to 1 week.

beverages

mulberry syrup

MAKES ABOUT **1½** CUPS [**360** ML]

2 cups [480 ml] fresh mulberry juice

1 cup [200 g] organic cane sugar, or more if needed

◆ Middle Easterners keep cool in the hot summers by drinking freshly pressed juices or iced drinks made with fruit syrups. The syrups are made by boiling down fresh fruit juice with sugar to produce a concentrated base that is then diluted with iced water and offered as an alternative to fresh juice. I remember my mother buying luscious mulberries in the summer from a vendor who knocked on our door carrying a huge enameled bowl full of the juiciest red mulberries I have ever seen. He would scoop the mulberries with a metal ladle and drop them into the large glass bowl my mother would hand him, sometimes splattering juice on her beautiful clothes. Once he had filled the bowl, my mother would pay him and then take the bowl into the kitchen, where she would give us children each a bowlful of mulberries to snack on before juicing the rest to turn into syrup. This we would drink once the season was over and sometimes also in winter if we felt like a taste of summer. I always keep a bottle of mulberry syrup in my refrigerator to make myself cool summer drinks, and whenever I do, I unfailingly remember the long, hot summers of my childhood and the beautiful red mulberry syrup drink swirling in my mother's crystal glasses.

As for the word *sharab*, it means "drink" in Arabic and it gave birth to *sharbat*, which became "sherbet" in English, to describe the drinks first devised by the Persians to replace the wine they could no longer drink under Islam. This recipe is for mulberry syrup, but the principle is the same for other berries that take your fancy—just make sure you choose them ripe. Also adjust the sugar according to the sweetness of the fruit. To make mulberry refresher, use about 3 Tbsp of this syrup per 1 cup [240 ml] of ice-cold water. Mix the water and syrup well before adding a couple of ice cubes to each glass.

continued

Mix the mulberry juice and sugar in a medium saucepan until the sugar dissolves and taste for sweetness. Some mulberries are sweeter than others.

Place the pan over low heat and let simmer until the juice is reduced to a medium-thick syrup, 15 to 20 minutes. Let cool.

Using a funnel, pour the syrup into sterilized glass bottles and seal. Store in a cool, dark place or in the refrigerator for up to 1 year.

fresh grape juice

MAKES ABOUT **3** CUPS [**720** ML]

2½ lb [1.2 kg] seedless green grapes, chilled

2 tsp orange blossom water

◆ I use green grapes to make this juice because I love their celadon color. Sometimes I serve juice made from both red and green grapes, alternating the glasses for color and flavor contrast. If you are not going to serve the juice immediately, make sure you refrigerate it in an airtight container so it does not oxidize, and don't keep it for longer than a day. Stir well before serving, as grape juice separates very quickly.

Pick the grapes off the stalks and process them through your juicer. If you don't have a juicer, process the grapes in a food processor and strain the juice, discarding the pulp.

Pour the juice into a pitcher, add the orange blossom water, and serve immediately.

pomegranate juice

MAKES **3** TO **4** CUPS [**720** TO **960** ML]

4½ lb [2 kg] juicy, sweet pomegranates, chilled and juiced

1½ Tbsp orange blossom water

◆ Throughout the Middle East there are fruit- and vegetable-juice stalls at every street corner, pressing juice to order for thirsty customers. You also find fruit-juice sellers wheeling carts through the streets, and if they are touting pomegranate or orange juice, their carts will be fitted with large metal citrus presses with a strong lever in which they press pomegranates the same way they would press oranges. Pomegranates range in color from a delicate pearly pink to a bright ruby red, depending on the variety. Just make sure you buy the sweet variety for juicing, not the sour, which is called *abu leffan* in Arabic, used in cooking and to make pomegranate syrup or molasses. It is difficult to predict how much juice you will extract from a pomegranate, so you should always buy a few extra.

There are two ways to extract the juice from the pomegranates. The quickest is to cut the fruit in half and press it like an orange. This can be a little messy, especially if you are pressing the fruit by hand and not using a press with a lever. Also, the pressed juice may have a hint of bitterness because of the white pith inside the skin. The other method is a lot more time-consuming, but will produce a juice that will taste a lot purer. Nonetheless, it is the method I use. Ease out the seeds by hand, and then process them through a vegetable juicer. An easier way to extract the seeds manually is to cut the pomegranate in half, turn the cut side over a bowl, and tap the skin with a knife. The seeds will drop into the bowl and you can then juice them in the vegetable juicer. If you don't have a juicer, use a food processor and strain out the pulp. If you are not going to serve the juice immediately, make sure you refrigerate it in an airtight container so it does not oxidize and don't keep it longer than a day.

Pour the pomegranate juice into a pitcher, stir in the orange blossom water, and serve immediately.

minty lemonade

MAKES **5** CUPS [**1.2** L]

⅔ cup [160 ml] freshly squeezed lemon juice

1 cup [30 g] mint leaves, minced, plus 4 sprigs fresh mint

4 cups [960 ml] water

¼ cup [50 g] superfine sugar, or more if needed

Ice cubes

◆ I first tasted this refreshing lemonade in Damascus nearly twenty years ago. Since then, the recipe has traveled, and it's available everywhere in Syria and in Lebanon as well. You can make it with limes for a different flavor, and you can add fragrance by adding a drop of orange blossom or rose water.

Put the lemon juice and mint leaves in a large pitcher. Add the water and sugar and stir until the sugar has completely dissolved. Taste for sweetness and add more sugar if you want your lemonade sweeter. Let infuse for about 30 minutes, and then strain out the mint.

Serve in glasses, with a couple of ice cubes and garnished with sprigs of fresh mint.

almond milk

MAKES **2½** CUPS [**600** ML]

2 cups [300 g] blanched almonds

½ cup [100 g] superfine sugar

2½ cups [600 ml] cool water

1 Tbsp orange blossom water

◆ I used to love commercial almond products like *crema di mandorle* (almond cream) and almond *horchata*—until a Moroccan cook taught me to make my own. The homemade version is rich and creamy with a luscious, fragrant taste. Almond milk makes a delightful nonalcoholic summer drink, and for those who are lactose intolerant, it is a great replacement for cow's or goat's milk to make ice cream or other milk-based desserts. If you find it too rich or too sweet, dilute it with a little more water.

Place the almonds in a heatproof bowl and pour in enough boiling water to cover. Let soak for 15 to 20 minutes. Drain well and put the almonds in a food processor. Add the sugar and 1 cup [240 ml] of the cool water; process until it forms a very fine paste.

Transfer the almond mixture to a mixing bowl, preferably one with a spout, and add the remaining 1½ cups [360 ml] water. Stir until the sugar has completely dissolved. Let infuse in the refrigerator for at least 30 minutes. Strain through a very fine sieve into a pitcher (if you don't have a very fine sieve, line a colander with cheesecloth and set the colander in a bowl). Press on the almond pulp to extract as much liquid as you can. Discard the almond pulp. Stir the orange blossom water into the almond milk. Store, covered, in the refrigerator for up to 3 days.

mint tea

SERVES 4

4 cups [960 ml] boiling water

2 tsp green tea leaves

3 Tbsp organic cane sugar

2 cups [50 g] fresh mint leaves

1 Tbsp pine nuts (optional)

◆ Middle Eastern hospitality is famous around the world. Even merchants in the souks will offer potential customers a cup of tea or coffee—perhaps to make the sale easier—but it's still a welcome gesture. In some countries, the drink will be tea; in others it will be coffee. In North Africa, mint tea is the drink of choice.

Tea making follows a ritual, with the man of the house always in charge. Traditionally, the tea is sweetened with pieces of sugar hacked from a cane sugar loaf that comes wrapped in gorgeous purple tissue paper, and the sugar is added to the pot rather than to the individual cups. If you prefer your tea without sugar, just omit it or decrease the quantity suggested. You can also use artificial sweetener. Tunisians often drop a few pine nuts into the tea glass—across North Africa tea is served in small beautifully decorated glasses—before pouring the tea. I love how the pine nuts soften as they sit in the hot tea, tasting as if they were fresh by the time you finally get to eat them.

Rinse a teapot with ¼ cup [60 ml] of the boiling water, pour off, and add the tea leaves. Add ½ cup [120 ml] boiling water and swirl it around a little before pouring the water out. (This was done in the old days to rinse the dust off the tea leaves. Although this step is unnecessary nowadays, I like the ritual so I still do it.)

Fill the pot with the remaining 3¼ cups [780 ml] boiling water and stir in the sugar. Crush the fresh mint a little with your hands, and add to the pot. Push the mint down into the liquid with a spoon. Leave to infuse for a few minutes. Serve in traditional tea glasses or teacups, dropping a few pine nuts into each glass if desired.

tea and coffee

Tea and coffee are the first sign of the legendary Middle Eastern and North African hospitality. In Iran, Morocco, Tunisia, and Algeria, the people drink mostly tea, while in Lebanon, Syria, and Jordan, coffee is the drink of choice. In Turkey and Gulf countries such as Qatar and the Emirates, both are imbibed. Turks grow tea in the Black Sea region but import their coffee; mostly from Yemen, whose coffee is favored not only by Turks but also by all Arab coffee drinkers. Gulf hosts serve both simultaneously for people to choose which they prefer, or even have one after the other. Whichever it is, great attention is paid to buying the beans or the tea leaves and to preparing the beverages.

While the people of the Maghreb (Morocco, Tunisia, and Algeria) favor green tea—imported from China and flavored with mint leaves, or absinthe in the winter—Iran and Turkey like black tea and grow their own.

The late shah's father was instrumental in switching his countrymen from coffee to tea drinkers. He strove to discourage coffee houses and their activities, which he deemed to be not so "innocent," and he imported new strains of tea from China together with families of farmers to oversee tea cultivation in Iran. He was successful in his endeavor to the point that Iran has now become a predominantly tea-drinking country with lush tea plantations in the north in the Caspian littoral. Iranians flavor their tea with cinnamon or dried rose petals for formal entertaining. The only time they drink coffee nowadays is at funerals or other solemn occasions.

iranian tea

SERVES 4

4 tsp Assam tea leaves

½ cinnamon stick, broken into 2 or 3 pieces

4 green cardamom pods, pounded in a mortar with a pestle

2½ cups [600 ml] boiling water

◆ Each Middle Eastern country has different ways of preparing tea, and each has a particular fondness for one type of tea leaf. Iranians use Assam tea, often flavoring it with spices. Iranians also prize their own local tea, which is grown on the northern slopes of Gilan province not far from the Caspian Sea. It is the custom in Iran to sweeten tea by sipping it through sugar cubes. Of course, you can also simply stir granulated sugar into the tea. This recipe is for a cinnamon and cardamom tea—a heady brew.

Put the tea leaves, cinnamon, and cardamom pods in a teapot. Add the boiling water and let infuse for a few minutes. Serve in typical Middle Eastern glass teacups.

Variation: You can vary the tea by substituting a few saffron threads, or by adding dried rosebuds and, just before serving, a few drops of rose water to enhance the fragrance. Dried limes are also used—use one dried lime for this recipe; quarter it and remove any seeds before letting it infuse for a few minutes with the tea leaves. Dried rosebuds and dried limes may be purchased from Kalustyan's (see Sources, page 162).

arabian tea

SERVES **2** TO **4**

1 cup [240 ml] whole milk

1⅓ cups [320 ml] water

1 tsp black tea leaves

2 tsp organic cane sugar, or more to taste

2 green cardamom pods, cracked open

¼ tsp ground cardamom

◆ The first time I had *karak* or *chai karak* was in Dubai, with an Emirati friend. *Karak* is similar to Indian chai—very milky, with a strong taste of cardamom. This strong, warming drink goes very well with many of the recipes in this book.

Put the milk and water in a saucepan and place over medium heat. Bring to a boil. Add the tea, sugar, and cardamom pods; let bubble for a couple of minutes. Turn the heat to low and let simmer for another 10 minutes. Add the ground cardamom and remove from the heat. Serve hot.

turkish coffee

SERVES **1**

¼ **cup [60 ml] water**
1 tsp finely ground coffee
½ to 1 tsp sugar

◆ When you visit a Lebanese home, your host or hostess will ask how you like your Turkish coffee, offering a choice between *murra* or *sada* (unsweetened), *wassat* or *mazbuta* (medium-sweet), and *hilwa* (sweet). The coffee is then "cooked"—always on top of the stove rather than brewed—to taste. The only time you will not be given a choice is if you are visiting for a sad or solemn occasion, in which case only unsweetened coffee is served. Mountain folk use cups with no handles, into which they pour a small amount of bitter coffee that they call *shaffeh*, meaning "one sip." Simply multiply the quantities given by the number of people to be served.

Pour the water into a *rakweh* (a special pot for making Turkish coffee; if you don't have one, simply use a small saucepan with a spout or a stainless-steel butter warmer). Place the pot over medium heat and bring the water to a boil. Stir in the coffee and sugar (½ tsp for medium-sweet, 1 tsp for sweet), turn the heat to medium-low, and wait until the coffee foams up. Remove from the heat as soon as the coffee starts rising up. Wait for it to settle, and then return to the heat. Remove as soon as the coffee foams up again and repeat another two or three times, until there is no more foam. Some people like their coffee quite foamy and stop after the first or second rise. Serve in demitasse cups.

arabian coffee

4 cups [960 ml] water

**3 Tbsp lightly roasted
ground coffee**

2 whole cloves

**1½ tsp to 1 Tbsp ground
cardamom**

**Good pinch of saffron
threads**

◆ Arabian coffee is very different from Turkish. The beans are roasted very lightly, whereas they are dark-roasted for Turkish coffee, and the coffee is boiled for a longer period, with the final result being a much lighter coffee in both color and taste. It is the only coffee that doesn't keep me up at night. I was given the following recipe by Aisha al-Tamimi, a wonderful Qatari TV chef and cookbook writer who (together with her sister Maryam Abdallah, the first Qatari TV chef) has taught me many Qatari specialties. Their first recommendation was that I should buy the coffee roasted one and a half times. When I pressed them for clarification, they just said that the shop where I buy the coffee will understand—perhaps in Qatar, but certainly not in England or America! Still, after insisting, Aisha and Maryam finally explained that the coffee needs to be lightly roasted so the beans remain blond (*ashqar*). A good coffee store should be able to accommodate your request for lightly roasted beans. Optional are the spices ground with your coffee. All the amounts are minimal, but Maryam asks for a little saffron, clove, and cardamom to be ground with her coffee. You can add spices to your plain ground coffee to achieve the taste you like. This coffee is usually served out of a pot with a long spout, called a *dalla*. The traditional way to serve it is to stack the cups in your left hand and hold the *dalla* in your right hand, lifting one cup slightly with your fingers to pour coffee into it and offer it to a guest. Cups should be refilled as soon as they are empty. The way to indicate you no longer need a refill is by shaking the empty cup in your hand before placing it on the table.

Pour the water into a saucepan, preferably one with a spout. Add the coffee and cloves and place over medium heat. Bring to a boil and let simmer for 10 minutes.

If you have a *dalla*, put the cardamom and saffron in it; if you don't, simply use a regular coffeepot or even a thermos. Pour the coffee over the spices, making sure you don't pour in any of the grounds. Let sit for 10 minutes. Serve in small round cups that have no handles—the same cups Lebanese mountain people use for *shaffeh* (see page 159).

sources

Kalustyan's

The place where you will find absolutely every single ingredient you will need for the recipes in this book. And if they don't have it, they will get it for you.

www.kalustyans.com
123 Lexington Avenue
New York, NY 10016
(212) 685-3451

Penzeys Spices

The source for an extensive selection of spices.

www.penzeys.com
Various locations

Phoenicia Specialty Foods

A wonderful Lebanese market with an excellent and wide selection of ingredients and an in-store bakery.

www.phoeniciafoods.com
12141 Westheimer Road
Houston, TX 77077
(281) 558-8225

Sadaf

An online store that offers a good, though not extensive, selection of ingredients from Lebanon and elsewhere in the Middle East.

www.sadaf.com

Sahadi's

An old-timer in Brooklyn with a fairly comprehensive selection of Middle Eastern ingredients.

www.sahadis.com
187 Atlantic Avenue
Brooklyn, NY 11201
(718) 624-4550

acknowledgments

First I would like to thank Celia Sack of Omnivore Books in San Francisco and her wife, Paula, who were both behind the birth of this book. A few years ago, I had wanted to do a book on Arab sweets but I worried about the calorie count as I tested the recipes, and I abandoned the idea. Then over dinner in London, Celia, Paula, and I discussed the idea of a book on Middle Eastern sweets; they urged me to do it, saying that the market was crying out for such a book. So I wrote a proposal, and Bill LeBlond at Chronicle Books, encouraged by Celia, commissioned it.

I would like to thank David Black, my agent, and Susan Friedland for her help with editing the manuscript. And a special thank-you to Amy Dencler for testing all the recipes so brilliantly to make sure they worked in a U.S. kitchen the way they had worked for me in my U.K. kitchen. I am also grateful to Amy for taking such good photographs of each recipe she tested so that I could see her results across the Atlantic. Thank you to Jane Levi, who also tested a few recipes, and to Jerome Henry, who perfected the delightful Saffron-Caramel Wafers.

I would like to thank Sheikha Bodour al-Qasimi of the United Arab Emirates for introducing me to Emirati food and for arranging to have the most wonderful ladies cook a wide range of dishes and sweets for me to taste and learn to prepare.

My appreciation goes out to my wonderful friends in Qatar, Aisha al-Tamimi and Maryam Abdallah, two sisters and eminent Qatari cooks. Most of what I know about Qatari food and sweets comes from them. I am also grateful to Nadia Mohamed Saleh, who sent me her mother's brilliant *sago* recipe.

Syria is a tragic story now, but before the uprising, I visited often to lead culinary tours and to see friends and family. The highlight of each trip was a visit to Pistache d'Alep, where the owners, Majed Krayem and Bassam Mawaldi, always received me with open arms. They had their sweets makers show me all their secrets, and every visit was thrilling. The same goes for the wonderful owners of İmam Çağdaş in Gaziantep, Turkey. Thank you to Filiz Hösükoğlu, my guru for all things in Gaziantep, and Hande Bozdoğan and Nevin Halıcı in Istanbul. Hande took me to what has become my favorite *kazandibi* place, and Nevin has taught me through her books, personal advice, and lovely companionship almost everything I know about Turkish food.

At Amal Bohsali in Beirut, my favorite place for *kunafa bil-jibn* and other sweets, I would like to thank Mr. Bohsali senior for inviting me to their kitchen and getting me an industrial quantity of soapwort root to experiment with in making *natef*. Also in Beirut, the late Hanna Mitri made the best-ever Arab ice cream, and even though he wouldn't part with his recipes, eating his ice cream was a revelation and helped me with the development of my own recipes. From Ozgüler in Gaziantep, who makes his wonderful ice cream with goat's milk, I learned to do the same.

A big thank-you to my very lovely mother, Laurice Helou, whose talent in the kitchen has been a constant inspiration, and whose knowledge and advice have been invaluable to me.

Finally, I would like to thank all the other people who have given me culinary inspiration and have helped make this book a reality. I am eternally grateful.

index